OLIVER CROMWELL
AND
THE PURITAN REVOLT

Failure of a Man or a Faith?

PROBLEMS IN EUROPEAN CIVILIZATION

UNDER THE EDITORIAL DIRECTION OF
Ralph W. Greenlaw* and Dwight E. Lee†

Other volumes in preparation

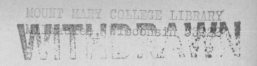

PROBLEMS IN EUROPEAN CIVILIZATION

OLIVER CROMWELL
AND
THE PURITAN REVOLT

Failure of a Man or a Faith?

EDITED WITH AN INTRODUCTION BY

Richard E. Boyer

UNIVERSITY OF TOLEDO

D. C. HEATH AND COMPANY · BOSTON

Englewood · Chicago · Dallas · San Francisco · Atlanta

Library of Congress Catalog Card Number 66–26809

Copyright © 1966 by D. C. Heath and Company

Printed August 1966

Table of Contents

Introduction

I N ONE of his speeches Oliver Cromwell spoke of his origin and the aims that he had set for himself. "I was by birth a gentleman, living neither in any considerable height nor yet in obscurity. I have been called to several employments in the nation, and . . . I did endeavor to discharge the duty of an honest man in those services to God and His people's interest, and to the Commonwealth." That he was a gentleman is generally conceded. As to his endeavors we must judge hereafter, for his character and his achievements are matters of great controversy; and about few other statesmen in history have so many conflicting judgments been expressed. Among the 30,000 pamphlets that tradition says this period produced, a multitude owed their origin to Cromwell; speeches, petitions, letters and sermons made him the best-known ruler of his time, yet he remains even today something of an enigma.

Cromwell's political ideals were the direct outcome of his religious creed. Political considerations were important in his life, but apparently of secondary importance. If he had a political mission it is hard to define precisely: "I can tell you, sirs, what I would not have, though I cannot what I would." What exactly did Cromwell mean when he spoke of "service to God?" If anyone had asked him what his duty was in public affairs, he would have answered that it was to do God's will. How does one determine God's will? Some Puritans claimed to have had it directly revealed to them, but not Cromwell. He said: "None climbs so high as he who knows not whither he is going." To him the interests of the people of God and the interests of the people of England may have been different but

definitely not irreconcilable. He felt that his government could reconcile the majority of the English people and win them to the interest of Jesus Christ.

In the attempt to carry out this policy Oliver Cromwell's career seems to contain a number of paradoxes, the most obvious one being that the revolutionary of the 1640's became the conservative dictator of the 1650's. He threatened to shoot the King if he had the chance and to exterminate all noblemen; and he certainly played the leading role in bringing Charles to the scaffold. He was, in short, the spokesman of the sectaries.

He organized the army to fight for Parliament against the King; he drew up and sponsored the Self-Denying Ordinance, which ordered all members of the two houses to resign their military commands, yet he retained his own command. He sided with the Army in every crisis: in December 1648 the Army purged Parliament, and in 1653 he used his own troops to dissolve that body. It was evident to many that he was able to assume the Lord Protectorship only as a result of his position as commander of the army. Yet from 1654 he aimed, with little success, at a settlement by which the military basis of his rule would end and a constitutional basis begin. He became a virtual monarch as he struggled to find a constitutional legitimacy, not necessarily a popular majority.

Even in his religious convictions, which he most strongly and genuinely held, there are obvious contradictions. Cromwell wrote to the General Assembly of the Kirk of Scotland: "I beseech you in the bowels of Christ, think it possible you may be mistaken," and said to the Governor of Edinburgh Castle, "Your pretended fear lest error should step in, is like the man that would keep all the wine out of the country lest men should be drunk." On the other hand he apparently justified the massacre of Irish Catholics at Drogheda as a "righteous judgment of God upon these barbarous wretches." It would be rather difficult to convince the Irish papists of Cromwell's toleration. He later said: "If by liberty of conscience you mean a liberty to exercise the mass, . . . where the Parliament of England have power, that will not be allowed."

Although not a hypocrite he sometimes appears to have come very near hypocrisy in implementing his policies. John Lilburne, admittedly not the staunchest admirer of the Lord Protector, wrote: "He will weep, howl and repent, even while he doth smite you under the first rib." The Levellers, with many of the other sectaries, naturally saw the Lord Protector as the schemer who "sacrificed the public cause to the idol of his ambitions." To them Cromwell had risen to power by promising to be loyal to their principles of a Commonwealth but had then gathered the reins of power into his own hands.

Many of these apparent contradictions stem from the political expediency of the day, but several also might be attributed to the Puritan ideals which guided the Lord Protector. The word "Puritan" has been the subject of much confusion and abuse. It certainly meant more than John Evelyn's definition given at the end of the Protectorate: "The religion of England is preaching and sitting still on Sundays." Another authority has defined Puritanism as "the religion of all those who wished either to purify the usage of the Established Church from the taint of Papacy, or to worship separately by forms so purified." Some maintain that it has no distinct theological meaning, but rather indicates a general attitude toward life which was found among many religious groups in England during the sixteenth and seventeenth centuries.

The debate over definition, to say nothing of interpretation, is still active.

The most heated controversy concerned problems of church government, but beneath these problems lay the vexing issue of predestination and free will. Calvinists generally tended to push the predestination principle to its radical extreme: there was no hope for anyone except those whom God had elected to be saved. The questions quite naturally arose: Who are the elect and who are the damned? On what grounds are they to be chosen or rejected? What can a man do, if anything, to be saved? The answer was that God alone determined from the beginning who would be saved and all one could do was to labor at his calling and hope to catch a glimpse of the divine will through his efforts to contribute to God's greater glory.

This basic doctrine of Puritanism, free will and eventually ultimate anarchy of individual conscience, seemed to Oliver Cromwell to justify military dictatorship as the only means of preserving the essential gains of the cause. He came to see himself as the unwilling instrument of the Puritan revolution. He was not only set over the people of England, but also over the "elect" of England; those with the "root of the matter." His was the obligation of leadership.

Oliver Cromwell's career illustrates the irreconcilable contradiction between ethics and politics, between the right and the expedient. The Lord Protector was consumed by an intense, narrow, burning patriotism, so closely interwoven with his religion that he could not distinguish one from the other.

With the exception of such poets as John Milton and Andrew Marvell, the recorded judgments of his contemporaries were hostile. Milton, however, identified Cromwell with his own cause:

Cromwell, our chief of men, who through a
    cloud
Not of war only, but detractions rude,
Guided by faith and matchless fortitude,
To peace and truth thy glorious way hath
    ploughed, . . .[1]

[1] "To the Lord General Oliver Cromwell."

Milton, occupying a position midway between the independents and the Levellers, believed in an aristocracy which would rule by the light of its wisdom and in accordance with natural law. He wanted complete separation of church and state and believed that it was impossible to have toleration as long as there was any state church at all. Despite his belief in the sovereignty of the people he had no faith in representative government. The opening selection in this volume, *Defensio Secunda*, represents an outstanding defense of Cromwell by Milton. Yet reading between the lines we discover that Milton's satisfaction was not unqualified. When the Commonwealth and Protectorate alike were over, Milton was silent and it remained for John Dryden to write:

His grandeur he derived from Heaven alone;
For he was great ere fortune made him so;
And wars, like mists that rise against the sun,
Made him but greater seem, not greater grow.[2]

In the main, the judgments of Cromwell's contemporaries were extremely critical. It was perhaps the Republicans who were the angriest. Their chief spokesman was Edmund Ludlow, one of Cromwell's former officers. Ludlow's dislike of Cromwell passed gradually into fanatical hatred; he turned conspirator and wrote incendiary pamphlets against the government. It was Ludlow's judgment that Cromwell had always wanted to be rid of Parliament and make himself king. With great bitterness Ludlow added: ". . . by the ambition of one man the hopes and expectations of all good men were disappointed." In his estimation the Millennium was at hand and Cromwell ruined the opportunity. He regarded the manifestations of Cromwell's Puritan spirit in politics as simply ludicrous. Cromwell is pictured as a rogue who deliberately donned a religious cloak as a means to satisfy his own ambitious ends.

Shortly after the Restoration, James Heath's *Flagellum* appeared, which Carlyle calls the "chief fountain of lies about Crom-

well." This work, long the most widely read of Cromwell's biographies went through six editions during the reign of Charles II. Heath, looking into Cromwell's background, allowed his subject no qualities except evil ones. Special attention is given to Cromwell's childhood and college days where, according to Heath, the football and cudgel seem to be Cromwell's study guides. The Protector emerges as a monster no less despicable in private life than damnable in public action and stripped even of common decency.

Ironically, the Royalists, whom he harmed the most, held him in higher esteem than the Republicans. Royalist historians of the Restoration period, witnessing the foreign policies of Charles II and James II, were wont to admit reluctantly that Cromwell's policy caused Britain to be respected and feared in the world of his time. Edward Hyde, the Earl of Clarendon, writing after his retirement from office, had mixed emotions about Cromwell, whom he viewed as possessing "all the wickedness against which damnation is pronounced and for which hell-fire is prepared" and yet "some virtues which have caused the memory of some men of all ages to be celebrated." Clarendon had never been an out-and-out royalist and was pushed by parliamentary extremists into a relationship with Charles I which lasted until the King's execution. He actually moved from being a moderate and critical Royalist to the spokesman of the Crown chiefly because of the excesses of the Long Parliament. He was sickened by enthusiasm in the cause of a rival creed, especially Puritanism, and he could not see Puritanism as a force which could link men together. Wrote Clarendon, "Cromwell had a wonderful understanding of the natures and humors of men . . . a great spirit, an admirable circumspection and sagacity, and a most magnanimous resolution"; he was, in short, a "brave, bad man."

If we consider Clarendon as representative of moderate Royalism, Mrs. Lucy Hutchinson represents extreme Puritanism.

[2] "The Death of Oliver Cromwell."

In the biography of her husband, Colonel Hutchinson, a prominent parliamentarian who signed Charles I's death warrant and later died in prison under Charles II, Cromwell is pictured not as doing "God's will" at all but as a vain and ambitious man who purposely thwarted Parliament, forsook his own religious ideals, and took over as a despot. According to Mrs. Hutchinson the Puritan leaders wanted a religious reform completely from the political situation. *The Memoirs of Colonel Hutchinson* gives us a glimpse of Oliver Cromwell the dictator rather than the Puritan defender of legal rights.

A second Puritan view is expressed by Richard Baxter, convinced opponent of Cromwell, who, while very critical of the role of the army, was determined to be just to the Lord Protector. According to Baxter, who has been described as the most learned and moderate of the Dissenters, Cromwell meant to do well and was pious until prosperity and success corrupted him after 1655. He adds almost apologetically: "It was his desire to do good . . . and to promote the interest of God more than any had done before him."

How does one explain this apparent paradox between Puritan ethics and Puritan politics? How could Oliver Cromwell transfer to secular politics the liberal elements in Puritanism while discarding the illiberal elements? Was Cromwell torn between religious ideals and the necessities of political action? Professor William Haller addresses himself to this point. Puritanism for Professor Haller was not the name of a definite body of religious doctrine or ecclesiastical system, but an attitude or point of view with regard to man's relation to God. He shows how its adherents saw themselves as clearly distinguishable from people with less exacting standards; and he suggests that as a result they were bound to feel that worldly social rank was relatively unimportant as compared to the essential equality of the elect. For Haller Puritanism was, in fact, nothing but English Protestantism in

its most dynamic form. He analyzes this complex dialectic subtly and sympathetically.

A well-rounded synthesis of the Puritan drive in England is ably presented by Professor Alan Simpson who extends his definition of Puritanism to include all points of view from Presbyterian to Quaker. It is, therefore, not difficult for him to deny that Puritanism was the monopoly of a single class. Simpson sees the Puritan phenomenon as fired by a powerful sense of fallen man in a fallen world. He describes the Puritan legacy with special attention to its impact on politics and leaves us with an excellent description of its virtues and limitations.

The late nineteenth and twentieth centuries witnessed the emergence of a "new breed" of biographers, one no longer obsessed with the urge to rewrite the seventeenth century as avengers of a dictator's victims or an annointed sovereign's blood. Samuel Rawson Gardiner, one of the greatest writers on the seventeenth century, is a member of this group. For Gardiner the truth had been obscured by the Whig or Tory biases of earlier historians. Despite his own Puritan background (as a descendant of Cromwell and Ireton through his paternal grandmother) Gardiner guarded partisanship by basing his work on primary sources wherever possible and using pamphlets and memoirs only occasionally. By Gardiner's time the approval of Cromwell's place in the triumph of middle-class virtues in a middle-class state was easily winning against condemnation of the rebel and tyrant. Gardiner advises us to use Cromwell as a mirror to look at our own weaknesses and strengths. Cromwell, according to Gardiner, faced an almost impossible task but was still the greatest Englishman because he was the "most typical." Gardiner maintains that after Cromwell's accession to power the Lord Protector applied his religious ideals in the national and social field. He made a conscious effort to govern in accordance with divine law and to follow God's will in all public and social relations. For Gardiner, Cromwell: "in the world of action was what Shakespeare was in the world of art, the greatest and most powerful Englishman of all time."

One of Professor Gardiner's disciples and admirers paid strict attention to the problem of portraying Cromwell's character. Professor Charles H. Firth's view of Cromwell is less imaginative but perhaps more sober than Gardiner's view. He makes much use of quotations and in these the full impact of Cromwell's personality is impressed upon the reader with almost contemporaneous force. In discussing Cromwell's policy of toleration, Firth makes the penetrating observation that "the liberality of Cromwell's practice often redeemed the comparative narrowness of his theory." It is typical of Firth's steady judgment, that in depicting Cromwell he gives due emphasis to the rational qualities of Cromwell's nature — his tolerance, his good sense, and his clearsightedness. Although Firth holds that religion was Cromwell's driving force, it is the practical man of affairs that emerges from the story rather than the mystic. Cromwell emerges as a statesman struggling toward a practical solution of fundamental political and religious problems. In such an interpretation we find little of the religious zealot or the dictator.

Perhaps the outstanding economic historian of the twentieth century, Professor R. H. Tawney emphasizes the economic rather than the religious drives behind Oliver Cromwell. In his admirable and absorbing work Tawney points out the remarkable coincidence of a particular religious affiliation with a particular social status, especially the identification of Cromwell with the industrial and commercial classes. Tawney pictures the world of business and society as a battlefield across which the Puritan could march triumphant to his goal. Relying a good deal on Baxter's *Autobiography*, Tawney discusses the narrow fanaticism of Puritanism and the demands it made for individual freedom.

Tawney's reliance on Baxter and his emphasis on economic issues is seized upon by Winthrop Hudson, noted Church historian, who criticizes Tawney for his very subtle but distorted characterization of Puritanism. Puritanism for Hudson was not necessarily a middle-class movement which rationalized and perpetuated middle-class ideals. He criticizes Tawney's excessive use of Baxter's *Autobiography* by pointing out that for Baxter property was not necessarily a sign of God's favor, nor was property evidence of his displeasure. Hudson maintains that for the Puritan, God was more important than business, property, pleasure, or any of the other aspects of life. He concludes that when Puritans became interested in these other aspects, they ceased to be Puritans.

At the other end of the spectrum Marxist historians ascribe great importance to the Cromwellian period, which to them is a "bourgeois revolution." To them it represents the political act by which English capitalism overthrew "feudal" society and insured for itself favorable conditions for development. The selection by Christopher Hill is a forceful presentation of the Marxist view by an outstanding English historian. Hill rejects any interpretation of the origin of the Commonwealth which ascribes this movement to religion or individualism. For the Marxists reality lies beneath both of these, in the successive stages of productive organization and in the rise and fall of classes. Hill maintains that the fact that Cromwell wrote and spoke in religious language should not prevent us from realizing that Cromwell represented a definite secular class: the bourgeoisie.

The final selection in this volume is by the noted historian and chairman of the Cromwell Association, Maurice Ashley. Writing in the 1930's Professor Ashley saw the Protector as a conservative dictator, but, as he himself later wrote, "I know more about Cromwell than I did then," and his emphasis in the selection presented here is quite different. Ashley presents the Pro-

tector in a new light. Seen against the
passionate religious and political movements
of seventeenth-century England, Cromwell
emerges as a military genius, a revolutionary who brought a king to the scaffold and
ruled England with a strong hand: "Oliver
Cromwell was a Christian by practice as
well as precept, a lover of his country, an
imperialist, who raised England to be a
Great Power." Discussing the achievements
of Oliver Cromwell and the Puritan Revolution, Ashley echoes the warning, however, that Cromwell should be seen not
through the colored spectacles of our own
emotions, but in the glaring light of his
own times.

Despite Dr. Samuel Johnson's comment
concerning Oliver Cromwell that "all that
can be told of him is already in print," the
fact remains that history cannot help being
concerned with people and that people as
individuals are interesting, to writers as
well as readers. Cromwell is certainly a case
in point. The offerings in this book represent only a sampling of the many views of

the Protector; and attempts to evaluate
Cromwell still provoke an occasional dispute.

Oliver Cromwell's problem was basically
one of trying to transform a military state
into a civil state. His career illustrates the
irreconcilable contradiction between the
practice and theory of politics which is the
eternal problem of statesmen. If his attempts were frustrated, it was because of
the impossibility of the task. He was unable to evolve a political system better than
the one he had destroyed. Most of his work
was swept away, but he made possible a
calm and almost bloodless return to the
monarchy and gave to England several
years of security and comparative prosperity after a period of civil war. Oliver Cromwell, in the words of his contemporaries,
was *politicus sine exemplo*. Was he from
the start a shrewd, far-sighted, cunning,
hypocritical, ambitious seeker after power,
or was he a product of his time and party,
led by circumstances and ability to the conduct of affairs? The reader must decide.

CHRONOLOGY

1599   Birth of Oliver Cromwell

1616   Admitted to Cambridge

1620   Married Elizabeth Bourchier

1628   Elected to Parliament from Huntingdon

1640   The Short Parliament is called and dissolved

1640   First session of the Long Parliament

1641   Execution of Strafford

1642   Charles I raises his standard at Nottingham

1643   The Solemn League and Covenant

1644   Marston Moor, the first important victory of Cromwell's Ironsides

1645   Battle of Naseby and the Self-Denying Ordinance

1646   Effective end of the First Civil War

1647   Departure of the Scots from England

1648   The Second Civil War and Pride's Purge

1649   The trial and execution of Charles I

1649   Establishment of The Commonwealth

1652   Outbreak of the First Dutch War

1653   Expulsion of the Rump Parliament

1653   The "Barebones" Parliament

1653   End of The Commonwealth and the establishment of the Protectorate

1653   Instrument of Government

1654   Peace with the Dutch

1655   Appointment of the Major Generals

". . . You suffered yourself, for the public good, a title most like to that of the father of your country. You did this not to exalt, but rather to bring you nearer to the level of ordinary men; the title of king was unworthy the transcendant majesty of your character."

— JOHN MILTON

"This kingdom was now almost stupified and tired out with the struggling against his government and domination, when it pleased God to call him to an account of all that mischief he had perpetrated; . . . And there he lodged and usurped a grave . . . taking his funeral triumphs for a more solemn cozenage of the executioner, till the due inevitable justice of heaven found him out, . . . which would have been so accomplished if this resolute destroyer had survived to that blessed time."

— JAMES HEATH

"He was not a man of blood, and totally declined Machiavelli's method; . . . In a word, as he had all the wickedness against which damnation is denounced, and for which hell-fire is prepared, so he had some virtues which have caused the memory of some men in all ages to be celebrated; and he will be looked upon by posterity as a brave bad man."

— EARL OF CLARENDON

"He at last exercised such an arbitrary power, that the whole land grew weary of him, while he set up a company of silly, mean fellows, called major-generals, as governors in every country. . . . Then he exercised another project to raise money, by decimation of the estates of all the king's party. . . . At last he took upon himself to make lords and knights, and wanted not many fools, both of the army and gentry, to accept of, and strut in, his mock titles."

— LUCY HUTCHINSON

"But how in particular, the unenlightened needed to know, do saints behave? The answer to this question the preachers dramatized in their own actions and then reduced to a code which they spread abroad in a hundred printed forms. The unloveliness of this code in some of its later manifestations should not blind us to its positive and bracing effect upon common life in Stuart times. . . . To the Puritans it seemed that the church was being used simply as a bulwark to protect privilege against reform."

— WILLIAM HALLER

"When the Puritan surveys the world within the terms laid down by Christian tradition, he is struck by the profundity of human sin, by the necessity for a work of grace in his own soul to redeem him from the lot of fallen humanity, and by the demand for a disciplined warfare against sin which

God makes on those he has saved. His pilgrimage is therefore a search for regeneration, which is usually achieved through an experience of conversion . . . ."

— ALAN SIMPSON

"It is time for us to regard him as he really was, with all his physical and moral audacity, with all his tenderness and spiritual yearnings, in the world of action what Shakespeare was in the world of thought, the greatest because the most typical Englishman of all time."

— S. R. GARDINER

"Cromwell's was the most tolerant government which had existed in England since the Reformation. In practice, he was more lenient than the laws, and more liberal-minded than most of his advisers. The drawback was, that even the more limited amount of religious freedom which the laws guaranteed seemed too much to the great majority of the nation. Englishmen — even Puritans — had not yet learnt the lesson of toleration."

— C. H. FIRTH

". . . the commercial and propertied classes were becoming increasingly restive under the whole system, at once ambitious and inefficient, of economic paternalism. It was in the same sections of the community that both religious and economic dissatisfaction were most acute. Puritanism, with its idealization of the spiritual energies which found expression in the activities of business and industry, drew the isolated rivulets of discontent together, and swept them forward with the dignity and momentum of a religious and a social philosophy."

— R. H. TAWNEY

"Cromwell should be seen not through the colored spectacles of our own emotions, but in the glaring light of his own times . . . the spirit and achievements of Oliver Cromwell were active elements in the revolution of 1688; they gave their impulse to a permanent form of English institutions; they largely attained their long-term objectives; and they may be said to have entered effectively into the making of modern England."

— MAURICE ASHLEY

I. CHARACTER OF THE PROTECTOR— CONTEMPORARY OPINION

God's Kingdom on Earth

JOHN MILTON

John Milton (1608–1674), outstanding Puritan spokesman and poet, identified early with the more radical group of Independents who under Cromwell's leadership were winning battles of the civil war. The trial of Charles I brought Milton into the political arena of public affairs and in 1649 he defended the sovereignty of the people in his "The Tenure of Kings and Magistrates," begun before the execution of the King and published immediately thereafter. For this Milton was made Secretary for Foreign Tongues to the new Council of State, an office he retained throughout the period of the Commonwealth and Protectorate. The duties included the drafting of state letters, translation, and the writing of political propaganda. The following selection was written after Milton was totally blind, in answer to the most libelous, and in some literary respects the ablest, attack that had yet been made upon Cromwell.

I NOW RETURN, as I promised, to produce the principal accusations against Cromwell; that I may show what little consideration particulars deserve, when the whole taken together is so frivolous and absurd. "He declared in the presence of many witnesses, that it was his intention to overturn all monarchies, and exterminate all kings." We have often seen before what credit is due to your assertions; perhaps one of the emigrants told you that Cromwell had said so. Of the many witnesses, you do not mention the name of a single one; but aspersion, so destitute of proof, falls by its own default. Cromwell was never found to be boastful of his actual exploits: and much less is he wont to employ any ostentatiousness of promise or arrogance of menace respecting achievements which were never performed, especially achievements of such difficulty. Those, therefore, who furnished

you with this piece of information must have been liars rather from spontaneous impulse or a constitutional propensity, than from deliberation, or they would never have invented a saying so contrary to his character and disposition. But the kings, whom you frequently admonish to take care of themselves, instead of accommodating their policy to the opinions which may be casually uttered in the street, had better enter on the consideration of the subject in a manner more suitable to its dignity, and more likely to throw light upon their interests. Another accusation is, that Cromwell had persuaded "the king to retire secretly to the Isle of Wight." It is well known that the affairs of Charles were often rendered desperate in other ways, and thrice by flight; first, when he fled from London to York; secondly, when he fled to the Scotch mercenaries in England; and

From John Milton, *John Milton An Englishman His Second Defence of the People of England against The Infamous Anonymous Libel, Entitled, The Cry of the Royal Blood to Heaven, against the English Parricides*. (London, 1654), pp. 100–108, 109–112, 126–128 (Editor's translation).

finally, when he retired to the Isle of Wight. But "Cromwell persuaded this last measure." This is to be sure beyond all possibility of doubt; but I wonder that the royalists should lavish such an abundance of praise respecting the prudence of Charles, who scarce ever seems to have had a mind of his own. For whether he was among his friends or his enemies, in the court or in the camp, he was generally at the disposal of others; at one time of his wife, at another of his bishops, now of his nobles, then of his troops, and last of all, of the enemy. And he seems, for the most part, to have followed the worst counsels, and those too of the worst advisers. Charles is the victim of persuasion, and is played upon, and is the pageant of delusion; he is intimidated by fear or deluded with vain hopes; and carried almost here and there, the common prey of every faction, whether they be friends or foes. Let them either erase these facts from their writings, or cease to extol the wisdom of Charles. It is an excellent thing to excell in prudence and in counsel, yet, when the country is torn with factions, it is not without its inconveniences; and the most discreet and cautious are most exposed to the more obnoxious factions. This often proved an obstacle in the way of Cromwell. Hence the presbyterians, his enemies, impute every harsh treatment which they experience, not to the parliament but to Cromwell alone. They do not even hesitate to ascribe their own indiscretions to the fraud and treachery of Cromwell; against him every invective is levelled, and it is he who must bear the blame of everything.

Indeed the flight of Charles to the Isle of Wight, which took place while Cromwell was some miles away, was so sudden and unexpected, that he acquainted by letter every member then in the city with the extraordinary occurrence. But this was the truth of the matter. The king, terrified by the army, which, neither softened by his requests nor his promises, had begun to demand his punishment, he determined to make his escape in the night with two trusty followers. But more determined to fly, than rightly knowing whither, he was induced, either by the ignorance or the timidity of his attendants, to make a voluntary surrender of himself to Hammond, governor of the Isle of Wight, in hopes of being able to procure a ship privately in order to sail to France or Holland. This is what I have learned concerning the king's flight to the Isle of Wight from those who possessed the readiest means of obtaining information. This is also one of the criminal charges: that "the English under Cromwell procured a great victory over the Scots." Not "procured," Sir, but, without any solecism, gloriously achieved. But imagine how bloody that battle must have been, the mere idea of which excited such trembling apprehensions, that you could not mention it without striking your head against Priscian's desk! But let us see what was the great crime in Cromwell in having gained such a complete victory over the Scots, who were menacing England with invasion, with the loss of her independence. "Amidst this confusion, while Cromwell is absent with his army": Yes, while Cromwell was engaged in subduing an enemy, who had marched into the very heart of the kingdom, and menaced the safety of the parliament: while he was employed in reducing the revolted Welsh to their obedience, whom he vanquished whenever he could overtake, and dispersed wherever he could find: the presbyterians "began to be tired of Cromwell." Here you speak the truth. While Cromwell is repelling the enemy at the hazard of his life, and bravely fighting in the field, they are conspiring to ruin his reputation at home, and suborn one Captain Huntington, to charge him with a capital offence. Who can ever listen to such ingratitude? By their instigation a mob of worthless people, reeking from the taverns and shops, besiege the doors of the parliament, and compel the members of that body by clamor and threats to vote such measures as they chose to dictate. And we should now have seen our Camillus, on his return from Scotland, after all his triumphs, and all his toils, either sent into banishment, or put to an ignominious death, if General Fairfax had not openly remonstrated against the disgrace of his invincible lieutenant; if the whole army, which had itself experienced a good deal of ill-treatment, had not intervened to prevent such atrocious conduct.

Entering the city, Cromwell quelled the citizens without much difficulty; they deservedly expelled from parliament those members who favored the hostile Scotch; the rest, delivered from the insolence of the rabble, broke off the conference which had begun with the king on the Isle of Wight, contrary to the express orders of the parliament. His accuser, Huntington, was left to himself; and at last, repented and of his own accord asked forgiveness of Cromwell, and confessed by whom he had been suborned. These are the principal charges, except those to which I have replied above, which are brought forward against this noble deliverer of his country. Of how little merit they are, you now see. But, in speaking of such a man, who has merited so well of his country, I should do nothing, if I only exculpated him from crimes; particularly since it not only so nearly concerns the country, but even myself, who am so closely implicated in the same infamy, show forth to all nations, and as far as I can, to all ages, the excellence of his character, and the splendor of his renown. Oliver Cromwell was sprung from a noble and illustrious family, who were distinguished for the civil functions which they performed under the monarchy, and still more for the part which they took in restoring and establishing true religion in this country. In the vigor and maturity of his life, which he passed in private, he was conspicuous for nothing more than for the strictness of his religious habits and the innocence of his life. He had cherished his confidence in God, he had nursed his spirit in silence for some time. When a parliament was at last called by the king, he was elected to represent his native town; and immediately became distinguished by the justness of his opinions, and the vigor and decision of his counsels. When the appeal was made to arms he offered his services, and was appointed to a troop of horse, whose numbers were soon increased by the eager zeal and the good, who flocked from all quarters to his standard; and in a short time he almost surpassed the greatest generals in the grandeur of his achievements and the rapidity with which they were performed.

Nor is this surprising; for he was a soldier disciplined to perfection in the knowledge of himself. He had neither extinguished, nor by habit had learned to subdue, the whole host of vain hopes, fears, and desires, which infest the soul. He first gained control of himself, and over himself acquired the most signal victories; so that on the first day he took the field against the external enemy, he was a veteran accomplished in all military duties. It is not possible for me in the narrow limits of this discourse to enumerate the many towns which he has taken, the many battles which he has won. The whole surface of the British empire has been the scene of his exploits, and the theatre of his triumphs; which alone would furnish ample materials for a history, and a space for narration equal to the things to be described. This alone seems to be sufficient proof of his extraordinary and almost supernatural virtue, that by the vigor of his genius, or the excellence of his discipline, adapted, not more to the necessities of war, than to the precepts of Christianity, the good and the brave were from all quarters drawn to his camp, and that during the whole war, and the occasional intervals of peace, amid many who opposed him he retained and still retains authority and the obedience of his troops, not by largesses or indulgence, but by his authority and the regularity of his pay. In this instance his fame may rival that of Cyrus, Epaminondas, or upon any of the great generals of antiquity. Hence he collected an army as numerous and as well equipped as any one ever did in so short a time; which was very well disciplined, and beloved by the citizens; which was formidable to the enemy in the field, but never cruel to those who laid down their arms; which committed no lawless ravages on the persons or the property of the inhabitants: who, when they compared their conduct with the violence, the intemperance, the impiety, and the debauchery of the royalists, were wont to salute them as friends, and to consider them as guests. They were a protection to the good, a terror to the evil, and the encouragers of piety and virtue. . . .

Without entering into any more detail, I will, if possible, describe some of the most memorable actions, with the same speed as you performed them. All Ireland was lost, with the exception of one city, as you in one battle defeated the forces of the rebels: and were busily employed in settling the country, when you were suddenly recalled to the war in Scotland. Hence you proceeded with unwearied diligence against the Scots, who were on the point of making an irruption into England with the King in their train: and in about one year you entirely subdued, and added to the English dominion, that kingdom which all our monarchs, during a period of 800 years, had been unable to subdue. In one battle you almost annihilated the remainder of their forces, which in a fit of desperation, had made a sudden incursion into England, then almost destitute of garrisons, and got as far as Worcester; where you came up with them by forced marches, and captured almost the whole of their nobility. There was at home a profound peace we found, though indeed not for the first time, that you were as wise in politics as valiant in war. It was your constant endeavor in the parliament either to induce them to adhere to those treaties which they had entered into with the enemy, or speedily to adjust others which promised to be beneficial to the state. But when you saw that the business was artfully contrived, that every one was more intent on his own selfish interest than on the public good, that the people complained of the disappointments which

they had experienced, and the fallacious promises by which they had been deceived, and that they were the dupes of a few overbearing individuals, you put an end to their sitting. A new parliament is summoned: and the right of election given to those to whom it was expedient. They meet: but do nothing; and, after having wearied themselves by their mutual dissensions, and fully exposed their incapacity to deal with the problems, they dissolve themselves. In this state of desolation, to which we were reduced, you, O Cromwell, alone remained to conduct the government and to save the country. We all willingly yield the sovereignty to your unrivalled ability and virtue, all but such, without equal ability are desirous of equal honors; or who know not that there is nothing in human society more pleasing to God, or more agreeable to reason; more politically just, or more generally useful, than that the supreme power should be vested in the best and wisest of men.

Such, O Cromwell, all acknowledge you to be; such are the services which you have rendered, as the leader of our councils, the general of our armies, and the father of your country. For this is the title by which all the good among us salute you from the very heart. Other titles you neither have nor could endure; and you deservedly reject that pomp of title which attracts the gaze and admiration of the multitude. For what is a title but a certain definite mode of dignity? Actions such as yours surpass, not only the bounds of our admiration, but our titles; and like the points of pyramids, which are lost in the clouds, they soar above the possibilities of titular honors.

But though it can add nothing to dignity, yet it may be expedient, for virtues, even the most exalted, should be circumscribed within some bounds. You suffered yourself, for the public good, a title most like to that of the father of your country. You did this not to exalt, but rather to bring you nearer to the level of ordinary men; the title of king was unworthy the transcendent majesty of your character. For if you had been captivated by a name, which, as a private man, you were able to subjugate, to reduce to a cipher, you would have been doing the same thing as if, after having subdued some idolatrous nation by the help of the true God, you should afterwards fall down and worship the gods which you had brought under subjection. Go on then, Cromwell, with your course of unrivalled magnanimity; it fits you well. Your own country's deliverer, nor can you sustain a character at once more momentous and more august than that of the author, the guardian, and the preserver of our liberties; and hence you have not only eclipsed the achievements of all our kings, but even those which have been fabled of our heroes. . . .

I pass by the rest, for who could recite the achievements of a whole people? If after such a display of courage and of vigor, you basely relinquish the path of virtue, if you do anything unworthy of yourself, posterity will sit in judgment on your conduct. They will see that the foundations were strongly laid; that the beginning, nay more than a beginning, was excellent; but it will be inquired with deep emotions of concern, who raised the superstructure and who completed the structure. To undertakings so grand, so virtuous, so noble, it will be a subject of grief that perseverance was wanting. They will see that there was a rich harvest of glory, and an opportunity afforded for the greatest achievements, but that men only were wanting for the work; while they were not wanting who could rightly counsel, exhort, encourage, and bind an unfading wreath of praise round the brows of the illustrious actors in so glorious a scene.

Hypocritical Tyrant

EDMUND LUDLOW

Edmund Ludlow (1617–1692) was a leading member of the Long Parliament and one of the chief promoters of Pride's Purge in 1648. After the execution of the King he asserted that the government under Oliver Cromwell was unlawful, and circulated pamphlets hostile to the Lord Protector. It was rumored that Ludlow was involved in several anti-Cromwell plots but he denied the charges. His memoirs say little about himself after 1667 and end abruptly in 1672. The history of the later part of his exile is very obscure. He went into exile in 1662 and died in Switzerland in 1692. The Mr. Peters referred to by Ludlow was Hugh Peters, an Independent preacher and leading pamphleteer who became the chaplain to the Model Army. During the Protectorate he was the regular preacher at Whitehall and after Restoration was arrested and executed.

ABOUT THE SAME TIME Mr. Peters, who still kept fair with those at Whitehall, made me a visit; and in our conversation about the public affairs I freely told him my opinion concerning the actions of Cromwell, endeavouring to make him sensible not only of his injustice, but great imprudence, thus to sacrifice the common cause to his ambition, and by every step he had lately taken to strengthen the hands

Charles H. Firth, ed., *The Memoirs of Edmund Ludlow, Esq., Lieutenant-General of the Horse in the Army of the Commonwealth of England, 1625–1672.* (Oxford, 1894), Volume II, pp. 8–12, 15, 18–19, 23–24, 28–29, 34–35, 37–38, 42–46.

of the common enemy, whereby he would undoubtedly open a way for the return of the family of the late king, who would not fail to do all that revenge could inspire them with: whereas if he had made use of his power to establish the just liberties of the nation, or could yet be persuaded so to do, he might live more honoured and esteemed, have the pleasure and satisfaction arising from so generous an action when he died, and leave his own family, together with the whole body of the people, in a most happy and flourishing condition. He confessed that what I had said was most true, but added, that there was not a man about him who had courage enough to tell him so: that for his part he had observed him immediately after the victory at Worcester to be so elevated, that he then began to fear what was since come to pass; and that he told a friend with whom he then quartered in his return to London, that he was inclined to believe Cromwell would endeavour to make himself king.

The usurper having governed as he thought long enough by virtue of the Instrument of Government, which though drawn up by himself and his creatures, was now thought to lay too great a restraint upon his ambitious spirit; and resolving to rest satisfied with nothing less than the succession of his family to the Crown, he attempted to make himself King. To this end he thought it necessary to call a Parliament: and that he might engage the army to assist him in all parts to procure such men to be chosen as would be fit for his purpose, he pretended that this assembly was called only in order to raise money for the payment of the army and fleet, to confirm the authority of the Major-Generals, and that of the Instrument of Government. By this means he obtained his desires in a great measure, especially in Scotland and Ireland, where all kinds of artifice, and in many places the most irregular courses, were taken to get such men returned as were proposed by the court. But knowing the people of England not to

be of so mercenary a spirit; and that as they were better instructed in the principles of civil liberty, so they were not wanting in courage to assert it, he used his utmost endeavours to disable and incapacitate such men from being chosen, whom he thought most likely to obstruct his designs. In order to do this he summoned the Lord President Bradshaw, Sir Henry Vane, Col. Rich, and myself, to appear before him in Council: which we all did except Sir Henry Vane, who told the messenger he should be at his house at Charing-Cross on a certain day. Cromwell, as soon as he saw the Lord President, required him to take out a new commission for his office of Chief Justice of Chester, which he refused, alleging that he held that place by a grant from the Parliament of England to continue *quamdiu se bene gesserit*.[1] And whether he had carried himself with that integrity which his commission exacted from him he was ready to submit to a trial by twelve English men, to be chosen even by Cromwell himself. Col. Rich being pressed to give security not to act against the Government, and refusing so to do, was sent prisoner to Windsor Castle. Then I drew near to the council-table, where Cromwell charged me with dispersing treasonable books in Ireland, and with endeavouring to render the offices of the army disaffected, by discoursing to them concerning new models of Government. I acknowledged that I had caused some papers to be dispersed in Ireland, but denied that they justly could be called treasonable. And though I knew not that it was a crime to debate of the several forms of Government, yet that I had not done any thing of that nature lately to the best of my remembrance. He then said, that he was not ignorant of the many plots that were on foot to disturb the present power, and that he thought it his duty to secure such as he suspected. To this I replied, that there were two duties required by God of the magistrate, i. e., that he be a terror to

---

[1] As long as I conduct myself well. [Ed. note]

those that do evil, and a praise to such as do well; and whether my actions were good or bad, I was ready to submit to a legal trial: that I was ignorant of any other way to secure the magistrate from being afraid of the people, or the people from the dread of the magistrate, unless both will do that which is just and good. "You do well," said he, "to reflect on our fears; yet I would have you know, that what I do, proceeds not from any motive of fear, but from a timely prudence to foresee and prevent danger: that had I done as I should, I ought to have secured you immediately upon your coming into England, or at least when you desired to be freed from the engagement you have given after your arrival; and therefore I now require you to give assurance not to act against the Government." I desired to be excused in that particular, reminding him of the reasons I had formerly given him for my refusal, adding, that I was in his power, and that he might use me as he thought fit. "Pray then," said he, "what is it that you would have? May not every man be as good as he will? What can you desire more than you have?" "It were easy," said I, "to tell what we would have." "What is that, I pray?" said he. "That which we fought for," said I, "that the nation might be governed by its own consent." "I am," said he, "as much for a government by consent as any man; but where shall we find that consent? Amongst the Prelatical, Presbyterian, Independent, Anabaptist, or Levelling Parties?" I answered, "Amongst those of all sorts who had acted with fidelity and affection to the public." Then he fell into the commendation of his own government, boasting of the protection and quiet which the people enjoyed under it, saying, that he was resolved to keep the nation from being imbrued in blood. I said that I was of opinion too much blood had been already shed, unless there were a better account of it. "You do well," said he, "to charge us with the guilt of blood; but we think there is a good return for what hath been shed; and we understand what clandestine correspondences are carrying on at this time between the Spaniard and those of your party, who make use of your name, and affirm that you will own them and assist them." "I know not," said I, "what you mean by my party, and can truly say, that if any men have entered into an engagement with Spain, they have no advice from me so to do, and that if they will use my name I cannot help it." Then in a softer way he told me, that he desired not to put any more hardships on me than on himself; that he had been always ready to do me all the good offices that lay in his power, and that he aimed at nothing by this proceeding, but the public quiet and security.

However, after this discourse and the conference of my relations with Serjeant Dendy, I ventured to accompany my father and mother Oldsworth, with my wife, into Essex, where we spent the remaining part of that summer. My stay there did in some measure answer the design of Cromwell, which was to keep me out of my own country, where he doubted I might obstruct the election of such persons as the Court had resolved by all methods to procure to be returned. But there was no need to fear my intermeddling in that particular at such a time; and if I had, it should have been only to give a public testimony against any election at all, the Long Parliament being still in being, though under a present force. Besides, it was manifest that the designed assembly was to be called for no other end than to strengthen the sword, and to advance the corrupt interest of him that called them together; and if it should happen that they had either the courage or honesty to attempt any thing for the service of the public, I was assured their endeavours would be rendered fruitless by a sudden dissipation.

. . . By this means, and the refusal of others to take out their permissions to sit from Cromwell and his council, as was required, lest they should seem to countenance such a detestable imposition and open breach of privilege, it came to pass that about a hundred of those who were elected by the country were excluded from the discharge of their trust, while those for Ireland and Scotland, who were chosen by and for the sword, were admitted without any scruple. Those that were excluded presented a petition to the sitting members, acquainting them, that being chosen by the country to serve with them, they were ready to discharge their duty, but were prevented from doing the same by the power of the sword, and refused admittance into the House by a guard of soldiers. After the petition had been read, a committee was sent to inquire of Cromwell and his council concerning the reasons of that proceeding, who returned with this answer: that if the persons complaining would address themselves to them, they should be relieved if there was cause. With this answer these men who would be counted an English Parliament acquiesced, leaving their privileges unvindicated, and the merit of elections to Parliament to be adjudged by men without doors. Then they proceeded to prepare divers bills, which tended chiefly to gratify the soldiery, and such persons as had received grants of land from Cromwell and his council, which were confirmed to them. Yet for all this harmony there were sometimes bitter reflections cast upon the proceedings of the Major-Generals by the lawyers and country gentlemen, who accused them to have done many things oppressive to the people, in interrupting the course of the law, and threatening such as would not submit to their arbitrary orders with transportation beyond the seas. . . . When the power of the Major-Generals came under consideration, all men were in great expectation concerning the issue of it. It was supposed that Cromwell, who had erected their authority, and engaged them in those actions for which they were now become odious, would support them against all attempts; because there appeared now no way so probable to maintain his own power, as by keeping the army firmly united to him. But ambition had corrupted his understanding to that degree, that he

made no scruple to sacrifice these men, who, to say no worse, had enlarged their consciences to an extraordinary size in the execution of his orders, to those who in requital of the favour had promised to make him King. . . .

Yet for all this he scrupled to take upon him the title of King, as a thing scandalous and of great hazard; though at the same time he vilified the former Instrument of Government to the last degree; and after having so highly magnified it when it was established he compared it now to a rotten plank, on which if a man set his foot it will break and leave him. The Assembly well understanding that the cause of his delays was either to be importuned to the thing, or to get time to persuade the army to be of the same opinion with himself, appointed a committee of their own members to give him their reasons for accepting this title. . . . But he was now arrived to that height of vanity, that though the design of this argument was only to persuade him to accept that which he desired above all things in the world; yet conceiving it below his grandeur to acknowledge such a prerogative in the Parliament alone, he expressed his dislike of it. And though he owned that the reasons they had offered had much weight in them, and that he was convinced there was no evil in the thing, yet he could not think it expedient to accept their offer, because he found that many of the good people of the nation were dissatisfied with it.

The grand design of the usurper having miscarried, the people were full of expectation to see what form of government the men of the sword would erect next. For as Cromwell had used all imaginable art and industry to throw dirt on all that had preceded, and most of all on the Instrument of Government, which he was once so fond of, and yet now alleged that it neither provided for the safety of the governors or governed: so the present Assembly had openly declared against the family of the Stuarts. But the restitution of the Commonwealth being the thing that was principally dreaded by these self-interested men, it was so contrived and carried, that the House shall present their Humble Petition and Advice to him again, with the sole alteration of the word King into that of Protector. This resolution was the more easily obtained, because the Commonwealth's men had been, under various frivolous pretences, denied their places in the Assembly; so that those only, who were for a Protector with an army, or those who were for King Oliver with an army, were the persons that were permitted to dispute within those walls. And now Cromwell having manifested his weakness, as well as his ambition in the late intrigue, was glad to take what he could get, and without any dispute agreed to what was proposed to him by the Assembly: which being done, the time was appointed for vesting him with the authority which was to be conferred upon him, and Westerminster-Hall was the place where the solemnity was performed. The aldermen of London and the judges, rather moved by fear than affection, were prevailed to be present; and Sir Thomas Widdrington, who was Speaker of the Assembly, was ordered to administer an oath to him, and to present him with a sword, a sceptre, and a Bible. The pretended Protector was clothed with a purple robe lined with ermine, the train of which was held by the son of the Lord Roberts. Of all the nobility the Earl of Warwick was the only person that accompanied him; and because he would still retain a form of godliness, he appointed Mr. Lockyer to preach before him at his return to Whitehall.

Cromwell having thus resumed the power into his own hands, made use of it to remove from the army such as he suspected to have obstructed his design; and beginning with his own regiment of horse, he sent for Col. Packer, who was the major, and Capt. Gladman, who commanded his own troops, with the rest of the captains of that regiment to attend him: whither being come, he demanded of them if they were willing to promise fidelity to the present Government, and to fight against those that should oppose it. They answered they were ready to fight against Charles Stuart, and that interest; but they could not engage against they knew not whom, and for they knew not what. But he, provoked with this answer, dismissed them from their commands, and placed men that would obey without reserve in their room. By this and other means he lost the affections of great numbers of men that would have been useful and faithful to him against the family of the late King. . . .

Cromwell having been disappointed, as I formerly mentioned, in his endeavours of procuring a civil authority to countenance his arbitrary power, made it his business so to balance all interests, that they should not dare to oppose him, for fear of bringing themselves into a worse condition than that wherein they were. To this end he gratified such of the Presbyterian party as were the most complying, and courted divers of the nobility, particularly the Earl of Warwick, whose grandson was admitted to be a suitor to his youngest daughter. . . .

After the death of Mrs. Claypole it was observed that Cromwell grew melancholy, and also distempered with divers infirmities, particularly a malignant humour in his foot; which hindering him from the exercises of walking or riding abroad, he obliged his physicians to endeavour to disperse it, which they endeavouring to do, drove it upwards to his heart. By this means he became desperately sick; and as some about him had for a long time deceived others, so they now endeavoured to impose upon God himself.

At Whitehall they were unwilling to have it known that he was so dangerously ill; yet by reason of a clause in the Humble Petition and Advice (which was the rule of Government they pretended to act by) that the Protector should have power to nominate his successor, the Commissioners of the Great Seal attended for signing the declaration of the person to be appointed to succeed him. But whether he was unwilling to discover his intentions to leave the succession to his son, lest thereby he should, in case of recovery, disoblige others, whom he had put in expectation of that power; or whether he was so discomposed in body and mind, that he could not attend that matter; or lastly, whether he would have named or did name any other, is to me uncertain. But certain it is that the Commissioners were not admitted till the Friday following, when the symptoms of death were apparent upon him, and many ministers and others assembled in a chamber at Whitehall, praying for him, while he manifested so little remorse of conscience for his betraying the public cause, and sacrificing it to the idol of his own ambition, that some of his last words were rather becoming a mediator than a sinner, recommending to God the condition of the nation that he had so infamously cheated, and expressing a great care of the people whom he had so manifestly despised. But he seemed above all concerned for the reproaches he said men would cast upon his name, in tramping on his ashes when dead. . . .

Different were the effects that the death of Cromwell produced in the nation: those men who had been sharers with him in the usurped authority were exceedingly troubled, while all other parties rejoiced at it: each of them hoping that this alteration would prove advantageous to their affairs. The Commonwealthsmen were so charitable to believe that the soldiery being delivered from their servitude to the General, to which they were willing to attribute their former compliances, would now open their eyes and join with them, as the only means left to preserve themselves and the people.

Man of Blood

JAMES HEATH

James Heath (1629–1664), Royalist pamphleteer and historian, was educated at Oxford but deprived of his studentship in 1648 by the parliamentarian visitors. An avid supporter of the King he went into exile with Charles II following Charles I's execution. Heath represents the extreme Royalist view of the Commonwealth. In addition to *Flagellum*, he is the author of the very biased *A Brief Chronicle of the Late Intestine Wars in the Three Kingdoms of England, Scotland, and Ireland* (1661).

I T WILL BE REQUISITE to speak something of his manner and course of life, now raised to a very near fruition of the sovereignty, this being the solstice of his fortunes. His custom was now to divert himself frequently at Hampton Court (which he had saved from sale, with other houses of the King for his own greatness) whether he went and came in post with his guards behind and before, as not yet secure of his life from the justice of some avenging band. Here he used to hunt, and at the fall of a deer, where he would be sure to be present, embrue his hands in the blood of it, and therewith asperse and sprinkle the attendants: and sometimes to coax the neighboring rustics, give them a buck he had hunted and money to drink with it;

From James Heath, *Flagellum: Or The Life and Death, Birth and Burial of Oliver Cromwell, The Late Usurper* (London, 1663), pp. 172–176, 180–181, 185–188, 192, 195, 202–203, 205–206, 212–213.

his own diet was very sparse and not so curious, except in public treatments, which were constantly given every Monday in the week, to all the officers of the army not below a Captain, where he dined with them, and showed a hundred antic tricks, as throwing of cushions, and putting live coals into their pockets and boots; a table being likewise spread every day of the week for such officers as should usually come to Court, and this was the greatest expense, which any other charges of the Government, he levied as yet by his council's ordinances, which were as duly and respectfully obeyed as Acts of Parliament.

With these Officers while he seemed to disport himself, taking off his drink freely, and opening himself every way to the most free familiarity, he did merely lie at the catch of what should incognantly and with such uninspected provocations fall from their mouths, which he would be sure to record and lay up against his occasion of reducing them to the speaker's memory, who were never like to forget the prejudice and damage they had incurred by such loose discoveries of their minds and inclinations.

. . . He had twenty other freaks in his head, for sometimes before he had half dined, he would give order for a Drum to beat, and call in his foot guards, like a kennel of hounds, to snatch off the meat from his table, and see them tear it in pieces; then like Joco's and Frisks he would have with other company; even with some few of the nobility, when he would not stick to tell them, what company they had lately kept, when and where they had drank the king's health and the royal families, bidding them when they did it again, to do it more privately and this without any passion, and as festiveness and droll discourse. . . .

The effects of this Parliament rupture encouraged two most opposite parties to conspire against the Protector, the Fifth Monarchists and Cavaliers (as we must so distinguish the Royal Party upon this difference, who) longed for their rightful sovereign Charles the Second, the Fifth Mon-

archy expected King Jesus, the Courtiers and those engaged by them or with them, with Cromwell himself, desired King Oliver and every one of these manifested much impatience, but none of them could attain their wishes, and when Oliver might afterwards he darest not, the Protector was no way ignorant of this, and therefore he resolved to deal with the weakest first, which yet by underminings was more dangerous than the others. The Army was corrupted by that millenary principle, and this was to be purged, so that as Harrison and Rich had been laid aside, and not long after committed with Carew and Courtney into several remote castles; so now General Monck had order to freeze Major General Overton, and the Majors Bramston and Holmes, and other officers, and cashier them, after fines and good security for their behaviour; Overton was sent up to the Tower, and his regiment conferred on Colonel Morgan; Coloney Okey's regiment taken from him, and given to a sure confidant and so the danger from the Army was quickly suppressed: Cornet but now Colonel Joyce, was likewise malcontent at this change, and signified so much to Cromwell's face, whom he upbraided with his own service and his faithlessness, but escaped any other censure than a bidding him begone; Cromwell well knowing him to be one of those mad men that would say or do any thing they were bid.

Now happened occasion, or rather Cromwell made it one, for him to show his zeal to the Protestant cause, and publish himself to the World the champion or Hector thereof; this was also one secret step and reach to the Crown, by invading the sacred title of the Defender of the Faith, due only to the hereditary sovereigns of England. Herein also he aimed, as in the proverb, to hit two birds with one stone, not doubting but to find another mint in the charitable minds and compassion of this nation towards the parallel suffering of the old Waldenses in Piedmont to the Irish massacres, which were set out and dressed here with the greater skill of butchery, then the actors could handsomely do it there, and it was said the copy was drawn from that original.

. . . For the better dispatch of this affair, he had erected a new military authority distributed into several Provinces of Counties, with an unbounded power, England being now cantoned. . . . The Commission was to take a roll and account of all suspected persons of the King's party, and such as were actually so to receive security of them, in which they were to be bound to act nothing against the Government, and to reveal all plots that should come to their knowledge: they were to suppress all horse-races, cock matches, and other concourses of people, to secure the highways, to take engagement from cavaliers, for their servants, and children, and those that did not so, nor give security to commit to prison, and to rate and receive the money rising from this decimation. In short there was nothing which they might not do; nor which they did not, such an arbitrary vast power they had from the Protector. To this purpose a Major General Office was erected in Fleetstreet, as other courts had, where these recognizances were entered, and all other the like affairs, dependencies, and concern thereof entered and recorded; by this means the tyrant intended to inform himself of the value and quality of every estate and person, together with the number of that party in every county throughout the kingdom. . . .

. . . From this haughty confidence he was invited to call another Parliament, and to assume from thence the long awaited result of his ambition, the Crown Imperial of England. All other things moreover did seem to conspire to the same purpose, except the Levelling Fifth Monarchy party, and Lambert: for the Presbyterian and other sectaries, who hid their hands full of sacrilegious and treasonable penny-worths, of ecclesiastical, and crown and delinquent lands, were most eagerly desirous of a settlement of the government by law, that might secure and confirm their purchases; the more indifferent Royalists preferred any legal (no matter how or what) authority, rather than be continually tasked and oppressed by the outrageous unlimited violence of the Major Generals, whom Cromwell had on purpose set up, as he did the little or foolish Parliament, to make another title be gaped at, more acceptable to the people.

As to the Fifth Monarchy men, he had nearly pried into that danger, and seized and took the chief of that party, among whom was Venner the wine-cooper, being engaged somewhat after in a plot, in a house in Shoreditch, where some arms were taken, and an Ensign with a Lyon merchant of the Tribe of Judah painted in it, having this Motto, Who shall raise him up?

And hereupon Harrison, Carew, Rich, Vice-Admiral Lawson, Courtney, Portman, Day, and the like, were imprisoned in remote places, as Col. Overton, Major Holmes, and others of the same party, had been seized in Scotland, and disbanded by General Monck, according to Cromwell's order, and sent up prisoners to the Tower of London.

As for the Levellers, he had lately discovered their practices and combinations against him, and had likewise locked up the chief of them, one Major Wildman, in order to his trial being taken at Marleborough, indicating and drawing declarations against him; so that they were at a stand and a loss which way to proceed, to the unsettling and overthrow of his tyrannical power; procured by so many tricks and cheats put upon them by him; so that afterwards when they be any private subscriptions to petitions, and addresses to the Parliament against the kingship, he peremptorily upon their peril forbid them to intermeddle with their consultations, and so awed and dashed them, that they never offered any more afterwards, to hold up so much as a finger against him. Lambert was the only impediment, and we shall see him neatly and quietly removed and discarded like the rest of his former confidants.

This Olivarian Parliament brought together by these means was not less awed in its election by the Major Generals (they themselves and all their friends being returned for members) while the gentry and other honest men being confined or under some qualification or other, could not, or dared not appear, particularly Col. Berkstead, and Kissing the Anabaptist. . . . The first work this parliament did was their declaring the justice of the war against Spain (the Cromwellian party personating the interest and honor of the nation, that they might be looked upon for all this garbling, as a due representative, and to credit their ensuing by-blowes) and a resolution to assist the Protector in it: and next as the grand and luminary work to Oliver's regality, An Act for the renouncing the title of His Majesty, and the whole Line of King James; seconded with another for the security of his highness in which they alleged the peace and safety of the nation was bound up.

And that this might appear most necessary and opportune, a plot was hatched by Cromwell and Thurloe, for further quashing all Levelling and Fifth Monarchy designs against that party; a book had likewise been lately divulged, styled, *Killing no Murder*, wherein it was proved, that it was most lawful, just, necessary, and honorable to kill him, and this printed with the name of one Allen a disbanded Leveller, but so politely and learnedly written, that it intimated a more exact and curious hand; whose ever it was, it scared Cromwell almost out of his wits, and made him betake himself to preventionary artifices, and fright assassinates with his severity against the suppositious authors of pretended dangers.

. . . We have through these labyrinths of his shifted designs, now eluded him to his lustful and adulterous usurpation, which the nocturnal pollutions of his dream had so long before fancied and acted in his thoughts.

This was the critical time, and the very juncture of his accomplishment of all his projections upon the Crown, which now seemed to court his brows by the complemental tender of a Parliament so picked and culled to his purpose. But it pleased God, to rescue the honor and majesty of England, from the profaneness of his temples; by some sudden emergent dangers, and suspicions he raised in his breast, and to elude his Royal phantoms with rival and democratic apparitions; his oracles now ceased, and a lying spirit was in the mouth of his prophets, who in their preachments harped upon this subject. Now that the reader may know how the whole mystery and cabal of this business was managed by the above mentioned committee (who would fain have drawn Oliver under the yoke of laws, and retrenched his exorbitant power of the sword) and Cromwell (who feared they would fortify his title, and weaken his tenure, and had noticed that Lambert labored in the debauch of the Army). He is here presented with the sum of that abortive regal consultation, which like the philosopher's stone, or rather the apples of Sodom, vanished and perished in the affectation.

. . . The Protector having refused the title of king (awaiting a more opportune time and advantage to reach to that top and height of his ambition, which inwardly tormented him) was now by the Parliament to be confirmed in his former dignity, and a Committee called of the settlement was ordered to prepare an explanatory part to the Humble Petition and Advice, in respect of the Protector's oath, his Councils, the members of Parliament, the other house, which was to consist of 60, and of Lords of Cromwell's election, of which in their place we shall give an account; all which with some acts being prepared and finished, the Protector came to the painted chamber, and sent for the Parliament, where the speaker tendered him these Acts of State, besides other relating unto trade, etc.

. . . He was now settled and established in his first assumed dignity, to the satisfaction of some part of the army, only Lambert was gravelled with that clause in it which gave the Protector power to name his successor. Whereby he saw himself deprived and frustrated of his hopes, and that contract that had passed between them. Cromwell therefore to secure himself, set the Army regiment after regiment to subscribe addresses congratulating his legal authority, and declaring their readiness to assert him therein with their lives and fortunes; being the very same method he had used before to prevent any designs against him in the army, when he was left upon his own bottom by the Parliament before.

. . . This kingdom was now almost stupefied and tired out with the struggling against his government and domination, when it pleased God to call him to an account of all that mischief he had perpetrated; ushering his end with a great whale some three months before on the second of June, that came up as far as Greenwich, and was there killed, and more immediately by a terrible storm of wind, the prognostic that the great Leviathan of men, that tempest and overthrower of government, was now going to his own place.

He was taken sick at Hampton-Court, having not been well in mind sometime before (troubled with the last frantic words of his beloved daughter Claypole, who threatened Judgement like another mad Cassandra, and with the insinuations and encroachments of the Republican party into the army, nor were most of his relations taint free of those principles, but were winding towards them): the disease was a bastard tertian which appeared not at first of any danger, but after a week's time it began to show very desperate symptoms, wherefore he was removed to Whitehall, where his chaplains and others of that pious family, kept private meetings and fastings of which they were so vainly confident (as before) that they obtruded their unseasonable thanks to God for the certainty of it, and with the same unseason-

able flattery with the Protector, deluded him into the like persuasion, so that he told his physicians, He should not die this bout; but the fits proving worse and worse, and causing him to talk idly, and to faint often. Continuing in this condition, he died on Friday the 3rd of September at 3 of the clock in the afternoon, though diverse rumors were spread, that he was carried away in the Tempest the day before: His body being opened and embalmed his milt was found full of corruption and filth, which was so strong and stinking, that after the Corpse were embalmed and filled with aromatic odours, and wrapped in cloth, six double, in an inner sheet of lead, and a strong wooden coffin, yet the filth broke through them all, and raised such a noisome stink, that they were forced to bury him out of hand; but his name and memory stinks worse.

. . . And there he lodged and usurped a grave (the impatient spectators fretting at this pompous mummery and magnificent cheat, taking his funeral triumphs for a more solemn cozenage of the executioner, till the due inevitable justice of heaven found him out, after the reduction of his sacred majesty in peace to his kingdoms, which would very difficultly have been so accomplished if this resolute destroyer had survived to that blessed time).

On the 30th day of January 1660, that day 12 years of his most nefarious parricide, his carcass with Bradshaw's and Ireton's, having been digged out of their graves, were carried to the Red Lyon in Holborn, and from thence drawn in sledges to Tyburn, where they hanged from ten of the clock in the morning till sunset, with their faces toward White-hall, and were then buried under the gallows, and his head set upon Westminster-Hall to be the becoming spectacle of his treason, where on that pinnacle and legal advancement it is fit to leave this ambitious wretch.

A Brave Bad Man

EDWARD HYDE, EARL OF CLARENDON

Edward Hyde, Earl of Clarendon (1609–1674), statesman and historian, became a member of the parliamentary opposition to Charles I, sitting in both the Short and the Long Parliaments in 1640. In January 1643 feeling that the king had granted all that could reasonably be expected Hyde left the opposition and gave his support to Charles. During the Civil War he was one of the king's most trusted advisers, and was made one of the councilors of Prince Charles. He assumed the office of Lord Chancellor of England and in 1661 was made Earl of Clarendon. As Charles II's chief minister Clarendon became increasingly unpopular at court and was dimissed from office in 1667. In October of that year he was impeached by the Commons, and in November he left England to spend the rest of his life in exile in France. He died at Rouen. He had begun his great historical work, "The History of the Rebellion," between 1646 and 1648 but completed it during his exile. It is far more accurate and impartial than one might expect, and his character portraits of the leaders on both sides are brilliant.

CROMWELL, though the greatest dissembler living, always made his hypocrisy of singular use and benefit to him; and never did any thing, how ungracious or imprudent soever it seemed to be, but what was necessary to the design; even his roughness and unpolishedness, which, in the beginning of the Parliament, he affected contrary to the smoothness and complacency, which his cousin, and bosom friend, Mr. Hampden, practised to all men, was necessary; and his first public declaration, in the beginning of the war, to his troop when it was first mustered, "that he would not deceive or cozen them by the perplexed and involved expressions in his commission, to fight for King and Parliament"; and therefore told them, "that if the King chanced to be in the body of the enemy that he was to charge, he would as soon discharge his pistol upon him, as any other private person; and if their conscience would not permit them to do the like; he advised them not to list themselves in his troop, or under his command"; which was generally looked upon as imprudent and malicious, and might, by the professions the parliament then made, have proved dangerous to him; yet served his turn, and severed from others, and united among themselves, all the furious and incensed men against the government, whether ecclesiastical or civil, to look upon him as a man for their turn, upon whom they might depend, as one who would go through his work that he undertook. And his strict and unsociable humour in not keeping company with the other officers of the army in their jollities and excesses, to which most of the superior officers under the earl of Essex were inclined, and by which he often made himself ridiculous or contemptible, drew all those of the like sour or reserved natures to his society and conversation, and gave him opportunity to form their understandings, inclinations, and resolutions, to his own model. By this he grew to have a wonderful interest in the common soldiers, out of which, as his authority increased, he made all his officers, well instructed how to live in the same manner with their soldiers, that they might be able to apply them to their own purposes: whilst he looked upon the Pres-

From G. D. Boyle, *Characters and Episodes of the Great Rebellion, Selected from The History and Autobiography of Edward, Earl of Clarendon* (Oxford, 1889), pp. 216–218, 277–284.

byterian humour as the best incentive to rebellion, no man more a Presbyterian; he sang all psalms with them to their tunes, and loved the longest sermons as much as they; but when he discovered that they would prescribe some limits and bounds to their rebellion, that it was not well breathed, and would expire as soon as some few particulars were granted to them in religion, which he cared not for; and then that the government must run still in the same channel; it concerned him to make it believed "that the State had been more delinquent than the Church, and that the people suffered more by the civil than by the ecclesiastical power; and therefore that the change of one would give them little ease, if there were not as great an alteration in the other, and if the whole government in both were not reformed and altered"; which though it made him generally odious [at first], and irreconciled many of his old friends to him; yet it made those who remained more cordial and firm: he could better compute his own strength, and upon whom he might depend. This discovery made him contrive the [new] model of the army; which was the most unpopular act, and disobliged all those who first contrived the Rebellion, and who were the very soul of it; and yet, if he had not brought that to pass, and changed a general, who though not very sharpsighted, would never be governed, nor applied to any thing he did not like, for another who had no eyes, and so would be willing to be led, all his designs must have come to nothing, and he remained a private colonel of horse, not considerable enough to be in any figure upon an advantageous composition. . . .

He was one of those men, *quos vituperare ne inimici quidem possunt, nisi ut simul laudent;*[1] for he could never have done half that mischief without great parts of courage, industry, and judgment. He must have had a wonderful understanding in the natures and humours of men, and as

great a dexterity in applying them; who, from a private and obscure birth, (though of a good family,) without interest of estate, alliance or friendship, could raise himself to such a height, and compound and knead such opposite and contradictory tempers, humours, and interests into a consistence, that contributed to his designs, and to their own destruction; whilst himself grew insensibly powerful enough to cut off those by whom he had climbed, in the instant that they projected to demolish their own building. What Vellieus Paterculus said of Cinna may very justly be said of him, *ausum eum, quae nemo auderet bonus; perfecisse, quae a nullo, nisi fortissimo, perfici possent.*[2] Without doubt, no man with more wickedness ever attempted any thing, or brought to pass what he desired more wickedly, more in the face and contempt of religion, and moral honesty; yet wickedness as great as his could never have accomplished those trophies, without the assistance of a great spirit, an admirable circumspection and sagacity, and a most magnanimous resolution.

When he appeared first in the Parliament, he seemed to have a person in no degree gracious, no ornament of discourse, none of those talents which use to reconcile the affections of the stander by: yet as he grew into place and authority, his parts seemed to be raised, as if he had had concealed faculties, till he had occasion to use them; and when he was to act the part of a great man, he did it without any indecency, notwithstanding the want of custom.

After he was confirmed and invested Protector by the humble petition and advice, he consulted with very few upon any action of importance, nor communicated any enterprise he resolved upon, with more than those who were to have principal parts in the execution of it; nor with them sooner than was absolutely necessary. When he once resolved, in which he was

---

[1] Not even his personal enemies can blame him, without praising him at the same time [Ed. note].

[2] He dared what no good man dared; he accomplished that which no one else accomplished, unless one was very brave [Ed. note].

not rash, he would not be dissuaded from, nor endure any contradiction of his power and authority; but extorted obedience from them who were not willing to yield it.

When he had laid some very extraordinary tax upon the city, one Cony, an eminent fanatic, and one who had heretofore served him very notably, positively refused to pay his part; and loudly dissuaded others from submitting to it, "as an imposition notoriously against the law, and the property of the subject, which all honest men were bound to defend." Cromwell sent for him, and cajoled him with the memory of 'the old kindness, and friendship, that had been between them; and that of all men he did not expect this opposition from him, in a matter that was so necessary for the good of the commonwealth." But it was always his fortune to meet with the most rude and obstinate behaviour from those who had formerly been absolutely governed by him; and they commonly put him in mind of some expressions and sayings of his own, in cases of the like nature: so this man remembered him, how great an enemy he had expressed himself to such grievances, and had declared, "that all who submitted to them, and paid illegal taxes, were more to blame, and greater enemies to their country, than they who had imposed them; and that the tyranny of princes could never be grievous, but by the tameness and stupidity of the people." When Cromwell saw that he could not convert him, he told him, "that he had a will as stubborn as his, and he would try which of them two should be master." Thereupon, with some terms of reproach and contempt, he committed the man to prison; whose courage was nothing abated by it; but as soon as the term came, he brought his *habeas corpus* in the King's Bench, which they then called the upper bench. Maynard, who was of council with the prisoner, demanded his liberty with great confidence, both upon the illegality of the commitment, and the illegality of the imposition, as being laid without any lawful authority. The judges could not maintain

or defend either, and enough declared what their sentence would be; and therefore the Protector's Attorney required a farther day, to answer what had been urged. Before that day, Maynard was committed to the Tower, for presuming to question or make doubt of his authority; and the judges were sent for, and severely reprehended for suffering that license; when they, with all humility, mentioned the law and magna charta, Cromwell told them, "their decisions should not control his actions; which he knew were for the safety of the commonwealth." He asked them, "who made them judges? whether they had any authority to sit there, but what he gave them? and if his authority were at an end, they knew well enough what would become of themselves; and therefore advised them to be more tender of that which could only preserve them"; and so dismissed them with caution, "that they should not suffer the lawyers to prate what it would not become them to hear."

Thus he subdued a spirit that had been often troublesome to the most sovereign power, and made Westminster-hall as obedient, and subservient to his commands, as any of the rest of his quarters. In all other matters, which did not concern the life of his jurisdiction, he seemed to have great reverence for the law, rarely interposing between party and party. As he proceeded with this kind of indignation and haughtiness with those who were refractory, and dared to contend with his greatness, so towards all who complied with his good pleasure, and courted his protection, he used a wonderful civility, generosity, and bounty.

To reduce three nations, which perfectly hated him, to an entire obedience to all his dictates; to awe and govern those nations by an army that was indevoted to him, and wished his ruin, was an instance of a very prodigious address. But his greatness at home was but a shadow of the glory he had abroad. It was hard to discover, which feared him most, France, Spain, or the Low Countries, where his friendship was current at the value he put upon it. As they did all sacrifice their honour and their interest to his pleasure, so there is nothing he could have demanded, that either of them would have denied him. To manifest which, there needs only two instances. The first is, when those of the Valley of Lucerne had unwarily rebelled against the duke of Savoy, which gave occasion to the Pope, and the neighbour princes of Italy, to call and solicit for their extirpation, and their prince positively resolved upon it, Cromwell sent his agent to the duke of Savoy, a prince with whom he had no correspondence, or commerce, and so engaged the cardinal, and even terrified the Pope himself, without so much as doing any grace to the English Roman catholics, (nothing being more usual than his saying, "that his ships in the Mediterranean should visit Civita Vecchia; and that the sound of his cannon should be heard in Rome,") that the duke of Savoy thought it necessary to restore all that he had taken from them, and did renew all those privileges they had formerly enjoyed, and newly forfeited.

The other instance of his authority was yet greater, and more incredible. In the city of Nismes, which is one of the fairest in the province of Languedoc, and where those of the reformed religion do most abound, there was a great faction at that season when the consuls (who are the chief magistrates) were to be chosen. Those of the reformed religion had the confidence to set up one of themselves for that magistracy; which they of the Roman religion resolved to oppose with all their power. The dissension between them made so much noise, that the intendant of the province, who is the supreme minister in all civil affairs throughout the whole province, went thither to prevent any disorder that might happen. When the day of election came, those of the religion possessed themselves with many armed men of the townhouse, where the election was to be made. The magistrates sent to know what their meaning was; to which they answered, "they were there to give their voices for the choice of the new consuls, and to be sure that the election should be fairly made." The bishop of the city, the intendant of the province, with all the officers of the church, and the present magistrates of the town, went together in their robes to be present at the election, without any suspicion that there would be any force used. When they came near the gate of the townhouse, which was shut, and they supposed would be opened when they came, they within poured out a volley of musket-shot upon them, by which the dean of the church, and two or three of the magistrates of the town, were killed upon the place, and very many others wounded; whereof some died shortly after. In this confusion, the magistrates put themselves into as good a posture to defend themselves as they could, without any purpose of offending the other, till they should be better provided; in order to which they sent an express to the court with a plain relation of the whole matter of fact, "and that there appeared to be no manner of combination with those of the religion in other places of the province; but that it was an insolence in those of the place, upon the presumption of their great numbers, which were little inferior to those of the catholics." The court was glad of the occasion, and resolved that this provocation, in which other places were not involved, and which nobody could excuse, should warrant all kind of severity in that city, even to the pulling down their temples, and expelling many of them for ever out of the city; which, with the execution and forfeiture of many of the principal persons, would be a general mortification to all of the religion in France; with whom they were heartily offended; and a part of the army was forthwith ordered to march towards Nismes, to see this executed with the utmost rigour.

Those of the religion in the town were quickly sensible into what condition they had brought themselves; and sent, with all possible submission, to the magistrates to excuse themselves, and to impute what had been done to the rashness of particular men, who had no order for what they did. The magistrates answered, "that they were glad they were sensible of their miscariage; but they could say nothing upon the subject, till the King's pleasure should be known; to whom they had sent a full relation of all that had passed." The others very well knew what the King's pleasure would be, and forthwith sent an express, one Moulins, a Scotchman, who had lived many years in that place, and in Montpelier, to Cromwell to desire his protection and interposition. The express made so much haste, and found so good a reception he first hour he came, that Cromwell, after he had received the whole account, made him "refresh himself after so long a journey, and he would take such care of his business, that by the time he came to Paris he should find it despatched"; and, that night, sent away another messenger to his ambassador Lockhart; who, by the time Moulins came thither, had so far prevailed with the cardinal, that orders were sent to stop the troops, which were upon their march towards Nismes; and, within few days after, Moulins returned with a full pardon and amnesty from the King, under the great seal of France, so fully confirmed with all circumstances, that there was never farther mention made of it, but all things passed as if there had never been any such thing. So that nobody can wonder, that his memory remains still in those parts, and with those people, in great veneration.

He would never suffer himself to be denied anything he ever asked of the cardinal, alleging, "that the people would not be otherwise satisfied"; which the cardinal bore very heavily, and complained of to those with whom he would be free. One day he visited Madam Turenne, and when he took his leave of her, she, according to her custom, besought him to continue gracious to the churches. Whereupon the cardinal told her, "that he knew not how to behave himself; if he advised the King to punish and suppress their insolence, Cromwell threatened him to join with the Spaniard; and if he shewed any favour to them, at Rome they accounted him an heretic."

He was not a man of blood, and totally declined Machiavel's method; which prescribes, upon any alteration of government, as a thing absolutely necessary, to cut off all the heads of those, and extirpate their families, who are friends to the old one. It was confidently reported, that, in the council of officers, it was more than once proposed, "that there might be a general massacre of all the royal party, as the only expedient to secure the government," but that Cromwell would never consent to it; it may be, out of too much contempt of his enemies. In a word, as he had all the wickedness against which damnation is denounced, and for which hell-fire is prepared, so he had some virtues which have caused the memory of some men in all ages to be celebrated; and he will be looked upon by posterity as a brave bad man.

II. FROM THE PURITAN POINT OF VIEW

To Promote the Interest of God

RICHARD BAXTER

Richard Baxter (1615–1691), English clergyman and writer, served as a chaplain in the Parliamentary army during the civil wars, but turned down service in Cromwell's regiment. He may be considered a moderate Presbyterian and worked toward the establishment of a universal Church which would include all true Christians. He helped to bring about the Restoration and despite persecution became a chaplain to Charles II. A prolific writer of over 150 works, his *Reliquiae Baxterianae* was completed in manuscript form about 1685 but not published until 1696. It is an admirable source of personal and historical information.

I COME NOW to the end of Cromwell's reign, who died (of a fever) before he was aware. He escaped the attempts of many that sought to have despatched him sooner, but could not escape the stroke of God when his appointed time was come (Though an independent, praying for him said, Lord we ask not for his life, for that we are sure of; but that he may serve thee better than ever he has done); to the dishonour of that presumption which some men call a particular faith; that is, a believing that they shall receive whatever they ask, if they can but steadfastly believe that they shall receive it, though it be such as they have no other premise for, but that of hearing, believing prayers, which they misunderstand.

Never man was highlier extolled, and never man was baselier reported of and vilified than this man. No (mere) man was better and worse spoken of than he, according as men's interests led their judgments. The soldiers and sectaries most highly magnified him till he began to seek the crown and the establishment of his family. And then there were so many tha would be half-kings themselves that a king did seem intolerable to them. The Royal ists abhorred him as a most perfidious hypo crite, and the Presbyterians thought hin little better in his management of publi matters.

If after so many others I may speak my opinion of him, I think that, having beer a prodigal in his youth and afterwar changed to a zealous religiousness, h meant honestly in the main, and was piou and conscionable in the main course of hi life till prosperity and success corruptec him; that, at his first entrance into the wars being but a captain of horse, he had a special care to get religious men into hi troop. These men were of greater under standing than common soldiers, and there fore were more apprehensive of the impor tance and consequence of the war, anc making not money but that which the took for the public felicity to be their end they were the more engaged to be valiant for he that maketh money his end dotl esteem his life above his pay, and therefor

From Richard Baxter, *Reliquiae Baxterianae: or Mr. Richard Baxter's Narrative of the Most Memora ble Passages of his Life and Times, Faithfully published from his own original manuscript*, ed. M Sylvester (London, 1696), pp. 98–105.

s like enough to save it by flight when danger comes, if possibly he can; but he that maketh the felicity of Church and State his end esteemeth it above his life, and therefore will the sooner lay down his life for it. And men of parts and understanding know how to manage their business, and know that flying is the surest way to death, and that standing to it is the likelist way to escape, there being many usually that fall in flight for one that falls in valiant fight. These things it's probable Cromwell understood, and that none would be such engaged valiant men as the religious. But yet I conjecture that, at his first choosing such men into his troop, it was the very esteem and love of religious men that principally moved him, and the avoiding of those disorders, mutinies, plunderings and grievances of the country which debauched men in armies are commonly guilty of. By this means he indeed sped better than he expected. Aires, Desborough, Berry, Evanston and the rest of that troop did prove so valiant that, as far as I could learn, they never once ran away before an enemy. Hereupon he got a commission to take some care of the associated counties, where he brought this troop into a double regiment of fourteen full troops, and all these as full of religious men as he could get. These, having more than ordinary wit and resolution, had more than ordinary success, first in Lincolnshire and afterward in the Earl of Manchester's army at York fight. With their successes the hearts both of captain and soldiers secretly rise both in pride and expectation; and the familiarity of many honest erroneous men (Anabaptists, Antinomians, etc.) withal began quickly to corrupt their judgments. Hereupon Cromwell's general religious zeal giveth way to the power of that ambition, which still increaseth as his successes do increase. Both piety and ambition concurred in his countenancing of all that he thought godly, of what sect soever. Piety pleadeth for them as godly, and charity as men; and ambition secretly telleth him what use he might make of them. He meaneth well in

all this at the beginning, and thinketh he doth all for the safety of the godly and the public good, but not without an eye to himself.

When successes had broken down all considerable opposition he was then in the face of his strongest temptations, which conquered him when he had conquered others. He thought that he had hitherto done well, both as to the end and means, and God, by the wonderful blessing of his providence, had owned his endeavours, and it was none but God that had made him great. He thought that if the war was lawful the victory was lawful; and if it were lawful to fight against the king and conquer him, it was lawful to use him as a conquered enemy, and a foolish thing to trust him when they had so provoked him (whereas, indeed, the parliament professed neither to fight against him nor to conquer him). He thought that the heart of the king was deep, and that he resolved upon revenge, and that if he were king he would easily at one time or other accomplish it; and that it was a dishonest thing of the parliament to set men to fight for them against the king, and then to lay their necks upon the block and be at his mercy; and that if that must be their case it was better to flatter or please him than to fight against him. He saw that the Scots and the Presbyterians in parliament did, by the Covenant and the Oath of Allegiance, find themselves bound to the person and family of the king, and that there was no hope of changing their minds in this. Hereupon he joined with that party in the parliament who were for the cutting off the king and trusting him no more. And consequently he joined with them in raising the Independents to make a faction in the Synod at Westminster and in the city, and in rendering the Scots and ministers as odious as he could, to disable them from hindering the change of government. In the doing of all this (which distrust and ambition had persuaded him was well done) he thought it lawful to use his wits, to choose each instrument and suit each means unto its end; and accordingly he daily employed himself, and modelled the army, and disbanded all other garrisons and forces and committees which were like to have hindered his design. And as he went on, though he yet resolved not what form the New Commonwealth should be moulded into, yet he thought it but reasonable that he should be the chief person who had been chief in their deliverance (for the Lord Fairfax, he knew, had but the name). At last, as he thought it lawful to cut off the king because he thought he was lawfully conquered, so he thought it lawful to fight against the Scots that would set him up and pull down the Presbyterian majority in the parliament, which would else, by restoring him, undo all which had cost them so much blood and treasure. And accordingly he conquereth Scotland, and pulleth down the parliament, being the easilier persuaded that all this was lawful because he had a secret bias and eye towards his own exaltation. For he (and his officers) thought that when the king was gone a government there must be, and that no man was so fit for it as he himself, as best deserving it, and as having by his wit and great interest in the army the best sufficiency to manage it: Yea, they thought that God had called them by successes to govern and take care of the Commonwealth and of the interest of all his people in the land; and that if they stood by and suffered the parliament to do that which they thought was dangerous, it would be required at their hands, whom they thought God had made the guardians of the land.

Having thus forced his conscience to justify all his cause (the cutting off the king, the setting up himself and his adherents, the pulling down the parliament and the Scots), he thinketh that the end being good and necessary, the necessary means cannot be bad. And accordingly he giveth his interest and cause leave to tell him how far sects shall be tolerated and commended, and how far not; and how far the ministry shall be owned and supported and how far not; yea, and how far professions, promises

and vows shall be kept or broken; and therefore the Covenant he could not away with, nor the ministers, further than they yielded to his ends or did not openly resist them. He seemed exceeding open-hearted by a familiar rustic-affected carriage (especially to his soldiers in sporting with them) but he thought secrecy a virtue and dissimulation no vice, and simulation — that is, in plain English, a lie — or perfidiousness to be a tolerable fault in a case of necessity; being of the same opinion with the Lord Bacon (who was not so precise as learned) that "the best composition and temperature is to have openness in fame and opinion, secrecy in habit, dissimulation in seasonable use, and a power to feign if there be no remedy." Therefore he kept fair with all, saving his open or unreconcilable enemies. He carried it with such dissimulation that Anabaptists, Independents and Antinomians did all think that he was one of them. But he never endeavoured to persuade the Presbyterians that he was one of them, but only that he would do them justice and preserve them, and that he honoured their worth and piety; for he knew that they were not so easily deceived. In a word, he did as our prelates have done, begin low and rise higher in his resolutions as his condition rose, and the promises which he made in his lower condition did require, and kept up as much honesty and godliness in the main as his cause and interest would allow (but there they left him). And his name standeth as a monitory monument or pillar to posterity to tell them. (The instability of man in strong temptations, if God leave him to himself: what great success and victories can do to lift up a mind that once seemed humble: what pride can do to make man selfish, and corrupt the heart with ill designs: what selfishness and ill designs can do to bribe a conscience, and corrupt the judgment, and make men justify the greatest errors and sins, and set against the clearest truth and duty. . . .

Cromwell being dead, his son Richard, by his will and testament and the army, was quietly settled in his place; while all men looked that they should presently have fallen into confusion and discord among themselves; the counties, cities and corporations of England send up their congratulations to own him as Protector (but none of us in Worcestershire, save the Independents, meddled in it).

He interred his father with great pomp and solemnity. He called a parliament, and that without any such restraints as his father had used. The members took the Oath of fidelity or allegiance to him at the door of the House before they entered. And all men wondered to see all so quiet in so dangerous a time. Many sober men that called his father no better than a traitorous hypocrite, did begin to think that they owed him subjection. They knew that the king was by birth their rightful sovereign; and resolved to do their best while there was hopes to introduce him, and defend him: But they were astonished at the marvellous providences of God, which had been against that Family all along, and they thought that there was no rational probability of his Restoration, having seen so many armies and risings and designs over them, which were raised or undertaken for it: . . . And I confess such thoughts were somewhat prevalent with myself: But God quickly shewed us the root of our error, which was our limiting the Almighty; as if that were hard to him that was impossible to us: So that the Restoration of the King, which we thought next to impossible, was accomplished in a trice: And we saw that twelve or eighteen years is not long enough to wait on God.

The army set up Richard Cromwell, it seemeth, upon trial, resolving to use him as he behaved himself; and though they swore fidelity to him, they meant to keep it no longer than he pleased them. And when they saw that he began to favour the sober people of the land, to honour parliaments, and to respect the ministers whom they called Presbyterians, they presently resolved to make him know his masters, and that it was they, and not he, that

were called by God to be the chief protectors of the interest of the nation. He was not so formidable to them as his father was, and therefore everyone boldly spurned at him. The Fifth Monarchy Men followed Sir Henry Vane, and raised a great and violent clamorous party against him, among the Sectaries in the city: Rogers and Feake, and such like firebrands preached them into fury, and blew the coals; but Dr. Owen and his assistants did the main work. . . . But if they would venture for their parts on new confusions, he would venture his part by retiring to his privacy. And so he did (to satisfy these proud distracted tyrants, who thought they did but pull down tyranny) resign the government by a writing under his hand, and retired himself, and left them to govern as they pleased. His good brother-in-law, Fleetwood, and his Uncle Desborough were so intoxicated as to be the leader of the conspiracy: And when they had pulled him down, they set up a few of themselves under the name of a Council of State; and so mad were they with pride, as to think the nation would stand by and reverence them, and obediently wait upon them in their drunken giddiness; and that their faction in the army was made by God an invincible terror to all that did but hear their names. The care of the business also was, that Oliver had once made Fleetwood believe that he should be his successor, and drawn an instrument to that purpose, but his last will disappointed him. And then the Sectaries flattered him, saying, that a truly Godly man that had commanded them in the wars was to be preferred before such a one as they censured to have no true Godliness.

I make no doubt but God permitted all this for good; and that as it was their treason to set up Oliver and destroy the king, so it was their duty to have set up the present king instead of Richard. And God made them the means to their own destruction, contrary to their intentions, to restore the monarchy and family which they had ruined. But all this is no thanks to them; but that which with a good intention had been a duty (to take down or not to set up Richard Cromwell) yet as done by them was a barbarous perfidiousness as most ever history did declare. . . .

The poor Church of Christ, the sober, sound religious part, are like Christ that was crucified between two malefactors; the profane and formal persecutors on one hand, and the fanatic dividing sectary on the other hand, have in all ages been grinding the spiritual seed as the corn is ground between the millstones . . . Yet there are few of them that lament their sin, but justify themselves and their misdoings, and the penitent malefactor is yet unknown to us.

O! what may not pride do? and what miscarriages will not false principles and faction hide? One would think that if their opinions had been certainly true, and their Church Orders good, yet the interest of Christ, and the souls of men, and of greater truths should have been so regarded by the dividers in England as that the safety of all these should have been preferred, and not all ruined rather than their way should want its carnal arm and liberty; and that they should not tear the garment of Christ all to pieces rather than it should want their lace.

And it must be acknowledged, also impartially, that some of the Presbyterian ministers frightened the sectaries into this fury by the unpeaceableness and impatience of their minds. They ran from libertinism into the other extreme, and were so little sensible of their own infirmity that they would not have those tolerated who were not only tolerable, but worthy instruments and members in the churches. The reconcilers that were ruled by prudent charity always called out to both the parties that the churches must be united upon the terms of primitive simplicity, and that we must have unity in things necessary and liberty in things unnecessary, and charity in all. But they could never be heard, but were taken for adversaries to the government of the Church, as they are by the prelates at this day. Nay, when in Worcester-

shire we did but agree to practise so much as all parties were agreed in, they said we did but thereby set up another party. . . .

When the army had brought themselves and the nation into utter confusion, and had set up and pulled down Richard Cromwell, Sir George Booth and Sir Thomas Middleton raised forces in Cheshire and North Wales (but the Cavaliers that should have joined with them failed them almost all over the land; a few rose in some places, but were quickly ruined and came to nothing). Lambert quickly routed those in Cheshire; Sir Arthur Haselrigge with Colonel Morley get into Portsmouth, which is possessed as for the Rump. Monk declareth against them in Scotland, purgeth his army of the Anabaptists, and marcheth into England. The Rump party, with Haselrigge, divided the army at home, and so disabled them to oppose Monk, who marcheth on, and all are afraid of him; and while he declareth himself against monarchy for a Commonwealth, he tieth the hands of his enemies by a lie and uniteth with the city of London, and bringeth on again the old ejected members of the parliament, and so bringeth in the king. Sir William Morrice (his kinsman) and Mr. Clarges were his great advisers. The Earl of Manchester, Mr. Calamy and other Presbyterians encouraged and persuaded him to bring in the king. At first he joined with the Rump against the citizens, and pulled down the city gates to master them; but at least Sir Thomas Allen, then Lord Mayor (by the persuasion of Dr. Jacomb and some other Presbyterian ministers and citizens, as he hath oft told me himself), invited Monk into the city, and drew him to agree and join with them against the Rump (as they then called the relics of the parliament). And this in truth was the act that turned the scales and brought in the king. Whether the same men expected to be used as they have since been, themselves, I know not. If they did, their self-denial was very great who were content to be silenced and laid in gaols so they might but bring in the king. After this the old excluded members of the parliament meet with Monk. He calleth them to sit, that the king might come in both by him and by them. He agreeth with them to sit but a few days and then dissolve themselves and call another parliament. They consented, and prepared for the king's restoration, and appointed a Council of State and dissolved themselves. Another parliament is chosen, which calleth in the king . . . And when the king came in, Colonel Birch and Mr. Prynne were appointed to disband the army, the several regiments receiving their pay in several places, and none of them daring to disobey; no, not Monk's own regiments who brought in the king.

Thus did God do a more wonderful work in the dissolving of this army than any of their greatest victories was which set them up. That an army that had conquered three such kingdoms and brought so many armies to destruction, cut off the king, pulled down the parliament and set up and pulled down others at their pleasure; that had conquered so many cities and castles; that were so united by principles and interest and guilt, and so deeply engaged, as much as their estates, and honour, and lives came to, to have stood it out to the very utmost; that had professed so much of their wisdom and religiousness, and had declared such high resolutions against monarchy — I say that such an army should have one commander among themselves, whom they accounted not religious, that should march against them without resistance, and that they should all stand still and let him come on and restore the parliament and bring in the king, and disband themselves, and all this without one bloody nose! let any man that hath the use of his understanding judge whether this were not enough to prove that there is a God that governeth the world and disposeth of the Powers of the world according to his Will! . . .

A Scheme of Aggrandizement

LUCY HUTCHINSON

Memoirs of the Life of Colonel Hutchinson, written by his wife Lucy Hutchinson, was not printed until 1806, 131 years after the probable date of Lucy's death. Intended simply for the preservation of his memory and instruction of his children, it possesses a peculiar value among seventeenth-century memoirs. Colonel Hutchinson (1615–1664) signed the death sentence against Charles I, retired into private life in 1653, and supposedly served the Royalist cause during the Protectorate. A moderate, he eventually wanted the restoration of the Long Parliament. At the Restoration Lucy Hutchinson exerted all her influence with her Royalist relatives to save the life of her husband, even venturing to write to the Speaker of the House of Commons. She overrates his political importance, it is true, and is prejudiced in her notices of his adversaries, especially Oliver Cromwell, but the *Memoirs* are unique as a representation of a Puritan gentleman.

AFTER THE DEATH of the king it was debated and resolved to change the form of government from a monarchy into a commonwealth, and the house of lords was voted dangerous and useless thereunto, and dissolved. A council of state was to be annually chosen for the management of affairs, accountable to the parliament, out

From *Memoirs of the Life of Colonel Hutchinson, Written by Mrs. Lucy Hutchinson from the Original Manuscript by the Rev. Julius Hutchinson* (London: 1806), pp. 303–305, 308–310, 335–343.

of which, consisting of forty councillors and a president, twenty were every year to go off by lot, and twenty new ones to be supplied. It is true, that at that time almost every man was fancying a form of government, and angry, when this came forth, that his invention took not place; and among these John Lilburne, a turbulent-spirited man, who never was quiet in anything, published libels; and the levellers made a disturbance with a kind of insurrection, which Cromwell soon appeased, they indeed being betrayed by their own leaders.

But how the public business went on, how Cromwell finished the conquest of Ireland, how the angry presbyterians spit fire out of their pulpits, and endeavoured to blow up the people against the parliament, how they entered into a treasonable conspiracy with Scotland, which had now received and crowned the son of the late king, who led them in hither with a great army, which the Lord of hosts discomfited; how our public ministers were assassinated and murdered in Spain and Holland; and how the Dutch, in this unsettlement of affairs, hoped to gain by making war, wherein they were beaten and brought to sue for peace — I shall leave to the stories that were then written; and only in general say that the hand of God was mightily seen in prospering and preserving the parliament till Cromwell's ambition unhappily interrupted them. Mr. Hutchinson was chosen into the first council of state, much against his own will; for, understanding that his cousin Ireton was one of the commissioners to nominate that council, he sent his wife to him, before he went to the house, that morning they were to be named, to desire him, upon all the scores of kindred and kindness that had been between them, that he might be left out, in regard that he had already wasted his time and his estate in the parliament's service; and having had neither recompense for his losses, nor any office of benefit, it would finish his ruin to be tied by this employment to a close and chargeable attendance, besides the inconvenience of his health,

not yet thoroughly confirmed, his constitution being more suitable to an active than to a sedentary life. These and other things he privately urged upon him; but he, who was a man regardless of his own or of any man's private interest, wherever he thought the public service might be advantaged, instead of keeping him out got him in, when the colonel had prevailed with others to have indulged him with that ease he desired. Mr. Hutchinson, after he had endeavoured to decline this employment and could not, thought that herein, as in other occasions, it being put upon him without his own desire, God had called him to his service in councils as formerly in arms, and applied himself to this also, wherein he did his duty faithfully, and employed his power to relieve the oppressed and dejected, freely becoming the advocate of those who had been his late enemies, in all things that were just and charitable. Though he had now an opportunity to have enriched himself, as it is to be feared some in all times have done, by accepting rewards for even just assistances, and he wanted not many who offered them and solicited him therein, yet such was his generous nature that he abhorred the mention of anything like reward, though ever so justly merited; and although he did a thousand highly obliging kindnesses for many, both friends and enemies, he never had anything in money or presents of any man.

Some of the army, being very desirous to get amongst them a person of whose fidelity and integrity to the cause they had such good experience, had moved it to the general, my Lord Fairfax; who commanded to have it inquired in what way he would choose to be employed; and when he told them that, in regard of his family, which he would not willingly be much absent from he should rather accept the government of some town than a field employment, four governments were brought to him, to select which he would have; whereof Plymouth and Portsmouth, and one more in the west, being at a vast distance from his own country, he made choice of Hull, in the north, though it was a less beneficial charge than the other, thinking they had not offered him anything but what had fairly fallen into their disposal. Soon after this, the lieutenant-general, Cromwell, desired him to meet him one afternoon at a committee, where, when he came, a malicious accusation against the governor of Hull was violently prosecuted by a fierce faction in that town. To this the governor had sent up a very fair and honest defence, yet most of the committee, more favouring the adverse faction, were labouring to cast out the governor. Colonel Hutchinson, though he knew him not, was very earnest in his defence, whereupon Cromwell drew him aside, and asked him what he meant by contending to keep in that governor? (it was Overton.) The colonel told him, because he saw nothing proved against him worthy of being ejected. "But," said Cromwell, "we like him not." Then said the colonel, "Do it upon that account, and blemish not a man that is innocent, upon false accusations, because you like him not." "But," said Cromwell, "we would have him out, because the government is designed for you, and except you put him out you cannot have the place." At this the colonel was very angry, and with great indignation told him, if there was no way to bring him into their army but by casting out others unjustly, he would rather fall naked before his enemies, than so seek to put himself into a posture of defence. Then returning to the table, he so eagerly undertook the injured governor's protection, that he foiled his enemies, and the governor was confirmed in his place. This so displeased Cromwell that, as before, so much more now, he saw that as even his own interest would not bias him into any unjust faction, so he secretly laboured to frustrate the attempts of all others who, for the same reason that Cromwell laboured to keep him out, laboured as much to bring him in.

But now had the poison of ambition so ulcerated Cromwell's heart, that the effects of it became more apparent than before,

and while as yet Fairfax stood an empty name, he was moulding the army to his mind, weeding out the godly and upright-hearted men, both officers and soldiers, and filling up their rooms with rascally turn-coat cavaliers, and pitiful sottish beasts of his own alliance, and other such as would swallow all things, and make no questions for conscience' sake. Yet this he did not directly nor in tumult, but by such degrees that it was unperceived by all that were not of very penetrating eyes; and those that made the loudest outcries against him lifted up their voices with such apparent envy and malice that, in that mist, they rather hid than discovered his ambitious minings. Among these, Colonel Rich and Commissary Staines and Watson had made a design even against his life, and the business was brought to the examination of the council of state. Before the hearing of it, Colonel Rich came to Colonel Hutchinson and implored his assistance with tears, affirming all the crimes of Cromwell, but not daring to justify his accusations, although the colonel advised him if they were true to stand boldly to it, if false to acknowledge his own iniquity. The latter course he took, and the council had resolved upon the just punishment of the men, when Cromwell, having only thus in a private council vindicated himself from their malice, and laid open what pitiful sneaking poor knaves they were, how ungrateful to him, and how treacherous and cowardly to themselves, became their advocate, and made it his suit that they might be no farther published or punished. This being permitted him, and they thus rendered contemptible to others, they became beasts and slaves to him, who knew how to serve himself by them without trusting them. This generosity, for indeed he carried himself with the greatest bravery that is imaginable herein, much advanced his glory, and cleared him in the eyes of superficial beholders; but others saw he creeped on, and could not stop him, while fortune itself seemed to prepare his way on sundry occasions. All this while he carried to Mr. Hutchinson the most open face, and made the most obliging professions of friendship imaginable; but the colonel saw through him, and forbore not often to tell him what was suspected of his ambition, what dissimulations of his were remarked, and how dishonourable to the name of God and the profession of religion, and destructive to the most glorious cause, and dangerous in overthrowing all our triumphs, these things which were suspected of him, would be, if true. He would seem to receive these cautions and admonitions as the greatest demonstrations of integrity and friendship that could be made, and embrace the colonel in his arms, and make serious lying professions to him, and often inquire men's opinions concerning him, which the colonel never forbore to tell him plainly, although he knew he resented it not as he made show, yet it pleased him so to discharge his own thoughts.

. . . Cromwell and his army grew wanton with their power, and invented a thousand tricks of government, which, when nobody opposed, they themselves fell to dislike and vary every day. First he calls a parliament out of his own pocket, himself naming a sort of godly men for every county, who meeting and not agreeing, a part of them, in the name of the people, gave up the sovereignty to him. Shortly after he makes up several sorts of mock parliaments, but not finding one of them absolutely to his turn, turned them off again. He soon quitted himself of his triumvirs, and first thrust out Harrison, then took away Lambert's commission, and would have been king but for fear of quitting his generalship. He weeded, in a few months' time, above a hundred and fifty godly officers out of the army, with whom many of the religious soldiers went off, and in their room abundance of the king's dissolute soldiers were entertained; and the army was almost changed from that godly religious army, whose valour God had crowned with triumph, into the dissolute army they had beaten, bearing yet a better

name. His wife and children were setting up for principality, which suited no better with any of them than scarlet on the ape; only, to speak the truth of himself, he had much natural greatness, and well became the place he had usurped. His daughter Fleetwood was humbled, and not exalted with these things, but the rest were insolent fools. Claypole, who married his daughter, and his son Henry, were two debauched, ungodly cavaliers. Richard was a peasant in his nature, yet gentle and virtuous, but became not greatness. His court was full of sin and vanity, and the more abominable, because they had not yet quite cast away the name of God, but profaned it by taking it in vain upon them. True religion was now almost lost, even among the religious party, and hypocrisy became an epidemical disease, to the sad grief of Colonel Hutchinson, and all true-hearted Christians and Englishmen. Almost all the ministers everywhere fell in and worshipped this beast, and courted and made addresses to him. So did the city of London, and many of the degenerate lords of the land, with the poor-spirited gentry. The cavaliers, in policy, who saw that while Cromwell reduced all by the exercise of tyrannical power under another name, there was a door opened for the restoring of their party, fell much in with Cromwell, and heightened all his disorders. He at last exercised such an arbitrary power, that the whole land grew weary of him, while he set up a company of silly, mean fellows, called major-generals, as governors in every county. These ruled according to their wills, by no law but what seemed good in their own eyes, imprisoning men, obstructing the course of justice between man and man, perverting right through partiality, acquitting some that were guilty, and punishing some that were innocent as guilty. Then he exercised another project to raise money, by decimation of the estates of all the king's party, of which action it is said Lambert was the instigator. At last he took upon himself to make lords and knights, and wanted not many fools, both of the army and gentry, to accept of, and strut in, his mock titles.

The cavaliers, seeing their victors thus beyond their hopes falling into their hands, had not patience to stay till things ripened of themselves, but were every day forming designs, and plotting for the murder of Cromwell, and other insurrections, which being contrived in drink, and managed by false and cowardly fellows, were still revealed to Cromwell, who had most excellent intelligence of all things that passed, even in the king's closet; and by these unsuccessful plots they were only the obstructors of what they sought to advance, while, to speak the truth, Cromwell's personal courage and magnanimity upheld him against all enemies and malcontents. His own army disliked him, and once when sevenscore officers had combined to cross him in something he was pursuing, and engaged one to another, Lambert being the chief, with solemn promises and invocations to God, the protector hearing of it, overawed them all, and told them, "it was not they who upheld him, but he them," and rated them, and made them understand what pitiful fellows they were; whereupon, they all, like rated dogs, clapped their tails between their legs, and begged his pardon, and left Lambert to fall alone, none daring to own him publicly, though many in their hearts wished him the sovereignty. Some of the Lambertonians had at that time a plot to come with a petition to Cromwell, and, while he was reading it, certain of them had undertaken to cast him out of a window at Whitehall that looked upon the Thames, where others would be ready to catch him up in a blanket if he escaped breaking his neck, and carrying him away in a boat prepared for the purpose, to kill or keep him alive, as they saw occasion, and then to set up Lambert. This was so carried on that it was near its execution before the protector knew anything of it. Colonel Hutchinson being at that time at London, by chance came to know all the plot. Certain of the conspirators coming into a place where he was, and not being so cautious of their whispers to each other before him, but that he apprehended something; by making use of which to others of the confederates, he at last found out the whole matter, without having it committed to him as a matter of trust, but which, carelessly thrown down in pieces before him, he gathered together, and became perfectly acquainted with the whole design; and weighing it, and judging that Lambert would be the worst tyrant of the two, he determined to prevent it, without being the author of any man's punishment. Hereupon, having occasion to see Fleetwood (for he had never seen the protector since his usurpation, but publicly declared his testimony against it to all the tyrant's minions), he bade Fleetwood wish him to have a care of petitioners, by whom he apprehended danger to his life. Fleetwood desired more particular information, but the colonel was resolved he would give him no more than to prevent that enterprise which he disliked. For indeed those who were deeply engaged rather waited to see the cavaliers in arms against him, which they thought would be the best time to arm for their own defence, and either to make a new conquest, or fall with swords in their hands. Therefore, they all connived at the cavaliers' attempts, and although they joined not with them, would not have been sorry to have seen them up upon equal terms with the protector, that then a third party, which was to be ready both with arms and men, when there was an opportunity, might have fallen in and capitulated, with swords in their hands, for the settlement of the rights and liberties of the good people: but God had otherwise determined things; and now men began so to flatter with this tyrant, so to apostatise from all faith, honesty, religion, and English liberty, and there was such a devilish practice of trepanning grown in fashion, that it was not safe to speak to any man in those treacherous days.

After Colonel Hutchinson had given Fleetwood that caution, he was going into the country, when the protector sent to search him out with all the earnestness and haste that could possibly be, and the colonel went to him; who met him in one of the galleries, and received him with open arms and the kindest embraces that could be given, and complained that the colonel should be so unkind as never to give him a visit, professing how welcome he should have been, the most welcome person in the land, and with these smooth insinuations led him along to a private place, giving him thanks for the advertisement he had received from Fleetwood, and using all his art to get out of the colonel the knowledge of the persons engaged in the conspiracy against him. But none of his cunning, nor promises, nor flatteries, could prevail with the colonel to inform him more than he thought necessary to prevent the execution of the design, which when the protector perceived, he gave him most infinite thanks for what he had told him, and acknowledged it opened to him some mysteries that had perplexed him, and agreed so with other intelligence he had, that he must owe his preservation to him: "But," say he, "dear colonel, why will not you come in and act among us?" The colonel told him plainly, because he liked not any of his ways since he broke up the parliament, being those which would lead to certain and unavoidable destruction, not only of themselves, but of the whole parliament party and cause; and thereupon took occasion, with his usual freedom, to tell him into what a sad hazard all things were placed, and how apparent a way was made for the restitution of all former tyranny and bondage. Cromwell seemed to receive this honest plainness with the greatest affection that could be, and acknowledged his precipitateness in some things, and with tears complained how Lambert had put him upon all those violent actions, for which he now accused him and sought his ruin. He expressed an earnest desire to restore the people's liberties, and to take and pursue more safe and sober councils, and wound up all with a very fair courtship of the colonel to engage with him, offering him anything he would account worthy of him. The colonel told him, he could not be forward to make his own advantage, by serving to the enslaving of his country. The other told him, he intended nothing more than the restoring and confirming the liberties of the good people, in order to which he would employ such men of honour and interest as the people would rejoice in, and he should not refuse to be one of them. And after he had endeavoured, with all his arts, to excuse his public actions, and to draw in the colonel, who again had taken the opportunity to tell him freely his own and all good men's discontents and dissatisfactions, he dismissed the colonel with such expressions as were publicly taken notice of by all his little courtiers then about him, when he went to the end of the gallery with the colonel, and there, embracing him, said aloud to him, "Well, colonel, satisfied or dissatisfied, you shall be one of us, for we can no longer exempt a person so able and faithful from the public service, and you shall be satisfied in all honest things." The colonel left him with that respect that became the place he was in; when immediately the same courtiers, who had some of them passed by him without knowing him when he came in, although they had once been of his familiar acquaintance, and the rest, who had looked upon him with such disdainful neglect as little people use to those who are not of their faction, now flocked about him, striving who should express most respect, and, by an extraordinary officiousness, redeem their late slightings. Some of them desired he would command their service in any business he had with their lord, and a thousand such frivolous compliments, which the colonel smiled at, and quitting himself of them as soon as he could, made haste to return to the country. There he had not been long before he was informed, that notwithstanding all these fair shows, the protector, finding him too constant to be wrought upon to serve his tyranny, had resolved to secure his person, lest he should head the people, who now grew very weary of his bondage. But though it was certainly confirmed to the colonel how much he was afraid of his honesty and freedom, and that he was resolved not to let him be any longer at liberty, yet before his guards apprehended the colonel, death imprisoned himself, and confined all his vast ambition and all his cruel designs into the narrow compass of a grave. His army and court substituted his eldest son, Richard, in his room, who was a meek, temperate, and quiet man, but had not a spirit fit to succeed his father, or to manage such a perplexed government. . . .

Set Up Your Banners in the Name of Christ

WILLIAM HALLER

William Haller (1885–   ), Emeritus Professor of English at Columbia University, was educated at Amherst and Columbia University. Specializing in English literature and history, Professor Haller has been a Fellow at the Folger and Huntington Libraries. He is the distinguished editor of several volumes of Puritan pamphlets and many scholarly articles as well as *Liberty and Reformation in the Puritan Revolution.* His observations are based upon his reading of the printed tracts, sermons, and other literature of the period over a lifetime of study.

Fɪʀsᴛ ᴏғ ᴀʟʟ we must endeavor to grasp the meaning of the central dogma of Puritanism as it applied to the life of men in the seventeenth century. This was a conception of an all-embracing determinism, theologically formulated as the doctrine of predestination. It is a conception which, especially in its postulates of an absolute human depravity and a purely arbitrary human redemption, has often seemed absurd to the common sense and abhorrent to the humanitarian sentiment of later generations. In these pages we are not concerned with such reactions. Believing in predestination, the Puritan preachers persuaded our forefathers to trust in nothing but God and the spirit within themselves and to defy the devil and all his minions. In doing this, they were not fools or clowns or bigots or pedants but academic intellectuals trained in the approved science and the accustomed arts of their time and addressing themselves to what they took to be the supreme need of the people of their time. With what ideas they could command they confronted the confusion and demoralization of a society which had been racked by the tremendous changes of the preceding century, and with what skill and force of character they possessed they attempted to implant courage, discipline and order. They took the doctrine of predestination as their dialectical weapon because it seemed to them to offer the most rational assurance for restored confidence in the future of mankind.

That Puritan doctrine was indebted to Calvin hardly requires to be said, but we have proceeded only a little way toward understanding the Puritan preachers when we have said that they were Calvinists. As Englishmen, they were Calvinists with a

From William Haller, *The Rise of Puritanism* (New York, 1938). Reprinted by permission of Columbia University Press, New York, pp. 83–85, 86, 89–91, 116–119, 123–127.

difference. In Geneva and in Scotland, as compared to England, the triumph of the Calvinist reformers had been quick and complete. Hence in those countries they soon gained a relatively free hand to impose their formula upon the whole social structure. No such opportunity to re-establish order throughout the church fell to the English Calvinists. Uniformity of belief and discipline was actually obtainable in England only within the sect or independent congregation and at the price of separation from the rest of society. The non-conformists and dissenters, though too weak and few to enforce their will upon others, did manage precariously to get their way among themselves, and those of them who were able to escape to New England were able to protect themselves from disunion if they wished by again handing heretics over to the secular arm or by turning them out into the wilderness. Thus in Geneva, in Scotland, in Massachusetts, and under peculiar limitations among the English sects, Calvinists of one type or another were able to achieve a reformed society in which differences of opinion were checked and uniformity maintained. But throughout England, except under the handicap of persecution, they were permitted to do nothing of the kind. There they had to accommodate themselves year after year as best they could to that peculiar condition which had been set up by the politic Elizabeth and which compelled Englishmen, the more surely the longer it endured, to the maintenance not of religious uniformity but of some sort and degree of toleration as the *sine qua non* of political security and economic prosperity. The reformers, then, unless they were willing to risk ostracism, exile or persecution, had to refrain from too directly assailing the government or their fellow subjects. They were in no position to suppress the people who did not fall in with their ideas, and had to advance their ideas as best they could by the peaceful arts of persuasion. Hence the English Calvinists found that all they could do to advance their cause, though they were for

some two generations permitted to do that, was to plead for it by the help of whatever gifts of mind and utterance they happened to possess. Under such conditions they produced, at any rate prior to 1640, no great public leaders, lawgivers and theologians of the stature of Knox and Calvin, but a host of popular propagandists who exploited as never before the potentialities of pulpit and press. Thus Calvinism in England did not lead to a swift reconstruction of the church but to the creation of a literature which expressed a way of life that eventually far transcended all ecclesiastical and even all religious bounds.

The history of Puritan thought in England is primarily the history of the setting forth of the basic doctrine of predestination in terms calculated to appeal to the English populace. It is at the same time necessarily a history of the effect of popular reaction upon the doctrine itself and upon the modes of its presentation. Strictly speaking, English Puritanism in the large may continue to be called Calvinistic chiefly as a matter of historical reference. Actually, the preachers, Calvinist though they were in varying degrees, referred as often to St. Augustine as to the author of the *Institutes*, but were chary on principle of citing any merely human authorities whatsoever. The French reformer's positive, clear, dogmatic intelligence supplied them with ideas but not on the whole with a model of discourse which they chose to imitate when they mounted the pulpit. . . .

The famous doctrine of predestination, of salvation by faith alone, was for the Puritan classes but the rationalized statement of this sentiment, a clear dogma answering with irrefutable logic to men's emotional need for something by which to be convinced. The modern mind, inexpert in such modes of reasoning, turns away from the intricate dialectic by which the logic of predestination was upon occasion presented, and we may well do the same here. The preachers themselves asserted again and again that only so much doctrine was important to be understood as could be understood by men of least knowledge and capacity when set forth in plain English. What, therefore, is important for us to understand is less how learned doctors argued among themselves than what they succeeded in conveying to the people, not what their doctrine was but what it meant and did.

The persuasive strength of the doctrine of predestination, as the Puritan preachers presented it, sprang not from its metaphysical but its moral validity. It could, men believed, be proved by inexorable logic out of scripture, but what really convinced them was its fruitfulness when applied to their own living situation. It was supremely apposite. It supplied a basis both practical and ideal for decision. It suggested an attitude and a line of conduct. Put to the test of experience, it applied and it worked. The concept of universal depravity, by leveling all superiority not of the spirit, enormously enhanced the self-respect of the ordinary man. If none were righteous, then one man was as good as another. God chose whom he would and the distinctions of this world counted for nothing. The concept of free grace still further heightened his confidence. If the only real aristocracy was the aristocracy created by God, then nothing really counted but character and inner worth. Only they were Jews who were Jews inwardly, and the true circumcision was not that of the body. If election were manifested not by outward conformity to an imposed law but by the struggle of the spirit within against the weakness and disobedience of the flesh, then any man might find reason for hope within his own breast. If all this was predestined, then there could be no fear concerning the issue of life's ordeal. "If God be with us, who can be against us?" The triumph of the saints was foreordained. Therefore nothing they could desire was impossible for them to attain. Heaven was theirs already, and if presently they demanded possession of the earth as well, that was no more than human.

Election, vocation, justification, sanctification, glorification, here was the perfect formula explaining what happened to every human soul born to be saved. It explained what happened to Paul, what might happen at any time to the very sinners who sat at the preacher's feet. The preacher could, of course, prove the formula to his own satisfaction beyond shadow of rational doubt. He could deduce it, that is, by an intellectual method which few of his hearers knew enough to question from premises which few men alive could critically examine. But it was far less important for his purposes to prove the formula than to demonstrate from observation and experience of life, as seen in himself, in the people about him and in the poetic narrative of scripture, precisely how it worked. In sermons and popular treatises almost beyond number, the Puritan preachers described the psychological pattern which exemplified the working of the formula, which all the saints were supposed to have exemplified and which every man who desired to be saved must hope would be exemplified again in his own case. As in later times men were taught to follow with patient observation the least workings of natural law in the external universe, men in the Puritan age were taught to follow by intense introspection the working of the law of predestination within their own souls. Theoretically, there was nothing they could do but watch, nothing they could of their own will do to induce or further the process of regeneration. They were only the witnesses of a drama which moved to its predetermined end according to a law they could do no more than marvel at. But the theatre of that drama was the human breast, and their own fate right up to the deathbed scene hung upon its outcome. They watched its unfolding, therefore, with the most absorbed attention. With the most anxious curiosity, they looked into their own most secret thoughts for signs that the grace of God was at its work of regeneration, and what they so urgently looked for they naturally saw. Seen by the light of the word, as they read it in the holy book and heard it expounded from the pulpit, their own lives fell under their gaze into the pattern set by Paul.

The preachers, though they had failed to win official recognition as leaders of public opinion, set themselves to gain the support of public opinion by living according to their principles in the public eye. Faith, we must remember, was the consequence, not the cause, of God's calling the soul to come out of sin. When faith was real, it manifested itself in the saint's persistence every hour of every day in every word and act of his life. He dwelt ever in his great taskmaster's eye.

But how in particular, the unenlightened needed to know, do saints behave? The answer to this question the preachers dramatized in their own actions and then reduced to a code which they spread abroad in a hundred printed forms. The unloveliness of this code in some of its later manifestations should not blind us to its positive and bracing effect upon common life in Stuart times. The merry England doomed by Puritan asceticism was not all cakes and ale, maypole dancing and frolics on the village green. We have but to turn to the picture which Baxter gives us of conditions in Cheshire and at Kidderminster to guess at the social chaos and moral corruption of many a swollen town and decaying country neighborhood. To the Puritans it seemed that the church was being used simply as a bulwark to protect privilege against reform. The traditional services, even when performed with dignity and beauty, appeared to them inadequate for the spiritual guidance of the people. Christian morality as well as Christian worship needed to be revitalized. This was what the preachers were endeavoring to effect, and the only question that can be raised is not as to the fact of their sincerity but as to the efficacy of their methods. They were endeavoring to adapt Christian morality to the needs of a population which was being steadily driven from its old feudal status into the untried conditions of competition between man and man in an increasingly commer-

cial and industrial society under a money economy. They seized upon the opportunities for communication afforded by the gathering of people in towns, by the rise of the press, and by the consequent spreading of literacy. That is, they had the pulpit and they had an audience which had the Bible. The humanitarian idealism of the gospels was, of course, not neglected in their sermons. But of even more practical application was the Hebrew code of conduct, interpreted and reinforced by the trenchant epitomizing genius of Paul. The preachers, consequently, recast for their own age Paul's digest of the laws of Moses, giving prominent place to the indispensable duties of Bible-reading and attendance upon sermons. Thus they offered a regimen which answered to a genuine longing on the part of many of the people for a more decent, more self-controlled and self-respecting existence.

Let us glance for a moment at the ideal day of the elect, as described in *A Garden of Spirituall Flowers* and the many other popular presentations of the Puritan code. The saint is told to awake with God and pray. "And let this bee done solemnely upon thy knees (and not as many doe, lazing upon their beds) that it may bee done with a humble, pure, and sincere devotion." If he is the head of a household, he should be stirring early to call his family together for morning prayers. After breakfast he may betake himself to his ordinary calling and business, seeing that his family does likewise. There are "Rules for the behaving of [himself] Christian-like in imployment about [his] worldly businesse, and enjoying the benefit of the same." He must keep close watch upon his heart, words and deeds, and see that his time is not idly, carelessly or unprofitably spent. He must mind his own business and let other men mind theirs. "Be not a Taleberer, nor a Tale-receiver: deale justly & uprightly with all men: let thy conversation be without covetousnesse, and without prodigalite: serve the Lord in singlenesse of heart: be doing good, and abstaine from all appearance of evill." In the same spirit he is told how to bear himself in company and in solitude, in prosperity and in adversity. He is not to shun prosperity nor yet to set his heart upon it. If it comes, it will come as God's free gift and is to be used as such. He is not to fear the adversity which God may bestow for the strengthening of his spirit. Business done, he goes home and concludes the day by gathering his household once more about him. He reads to them from scripture, catechizes them, sings psalms and prays with them. Then he goes to his chamber to meditate and, as we have seen, to balance his spiritual accounts. And so to bed. For Sundays, he is given special directions. In church, whither he proceeds in the morning at the head of his family, he must keep his eyes fixed on the preacher, so that his thoughts may not wander. He is advised to mark the speaker's text, observe how it is "divided," note the handling of each division, find the places in scripture alleged for proof, fold down the leaf at the appropriate passages so that he may review them at leisure. Then home again to discuss the sermon with the family after dinner and back again to church to repeat the whole performance in the afternoon. If such a program seem preposterous to the man of the present day, he should remember that his forefathers even in the conduct of this world's business were concerned about their consciences. Perhaps the desire of later generations to escape from Puritanism has been at least in part a desire to do business with less hindrance from a scheme of life so insistent upon keeping the individual forever in mind of his moral responsibilities.

One further aspect of the Puritan conception of the good life remains to be presented before we undertake to discuss the saga of the spiritual life set forth in the sermons. The preachers endeavored by precept and example to show how the elect, while living according to the code of saintliness, must use their gifts and opportunities in this life. The Puritan code was much more than a table of prohibitions. It was the program of an active, not a monastic or contemplative, life. The saints stripped themselves for battle, and only as the battle waxed hot and desperate did they degenerate into the fanatical iconoclasts of familiar tradition. Milton's lady scorned not the gifts that Comus offered her but the giver. "Worldly things," according to Sibbes, "are good in themselves, and given to sweeten our passage to Heaven," even to sweeten our "profession of Religion." We must use the world as our servant, not our master, take comfort in it but not set our hearts upon it or let ourselves be made "drunke with the cares below." All is, in other words, as we have grace to use it. "This world and the things thereof are all good, and were all made of God, for the benefit of his creature." John Dod, gathering his flock about him, opening his doors to all comers, sitting down at the head of a full table, talking himself thirsty, and calling for a draft of wine and beer mixed, was no bigoted ascetic, though he did disapprove of stage plays, dancing and card-playing. The saint had no reason to fear the world or run away from it. Rather he must go forth into it and do the will of God there. Rogers scorns the suggestion that, if men live according to the godly rule, they will neglect their necessary affairs "and so poverty grow upon the land." On the contrary, he says, "he who goes about it preposterously, & shal find his successe answerable." "He riddeth not most worke, who goeth to it most early, when his instruments which he should use in the performance of the same be blunt and dull." "Godlinesse hinders not mens labours, neither decaies the Common-wealth." There is a "godly thrift," a "Christian gaining" and a "lawfull prospering" which come to him who goes to work "with a minde which is at peace with God." Who cannot see that by the labor of such men "the Common-wealth . . . should flourish much more, having a certeine promise of blessing"?

The saint knows that he need not fear to lose a penny while he stops to say his prayers. He knows that whatever he has and whatever he gains in the course of business comes from God. His prime piece of capital, he knows, consists in the abilities and opportunities which God has bestowed upon him for doing the business of the world. They are his talent, and he never forgets by whom this was given or by whom and on what terms it will be exacted in return. This doctrine comes, of course, directly from the parable of the talents, "wherein," to use the words of Gabriel Powell, "is shewed, that no man, of what state or condition soever hee bee, is Lord of his owne riches or substance, but the steward and disposer of it, accountable unto God for all things." It is the theme of Milton's sonnet concerning the one talent which is death to hide. Our individual abilities are not given us as rewards to be enjoyed — no sinner merits any favor from God. Nor does God grant them as necessary means to ends of his own — "God doth not need either man's work or his own gifts." They are bestowed as unconditioned occasions for service upon such as truly love their maker. Those who put their gifts to work, or, as Milton would have it, merely stand ready and waiting to do so, may feel assured that they please him. Those who do not may expect one day to hear the master chide. For, to quote Powell once more, "we must be accountable for the least farthing which we have received of God; after what manner we came by it, how and to what use we have bestowed and spent it."

No part of the Puritan code was more weighted with practical significance than this. Nothing in the postulates of Puritan doctrine up to this point was inconsistent with the stopping of Puritanism at mere pietism within self-centered groups of believers, and such pietistic groups did in fact spring up within the Puritan movement as among Protestants on the continent. But by insistence upon the moral aspects of the doctrine of the talent the preachers opened a wide door through which they drove their flocks out into the world to have their fill of experience. To be specific, they gave

in this way to the general doctrine of God's calling a definite application. When God called his elect to repent and believe, he also called upon them to act. The gifts and opportunities, no matter how humble and narrow, with which the saint was invested were also part of his commission from God. Whatsoever we undertake in the exercise of our talents and in the spirit of faith is good. It is what God has called us to do. Woe unto us if we do not do it, and happy the man who responds to the vocation of his own abilities. God is strict about his business, but just. "They which are furnished with gifts for their callings, namely aptnesse and willingnesse, and are thereunto called or set apart by men" may rest assured that they are called by God. Moreover, when they walk in a calling lawful in itself and suited to their capacities, they are walking in his presence and under his special protection. This was a conviction destined to have disturbing results when authority attempted to rule that it was not lawful for a Milton to exercise his talent for instructing his fellow countrymen or a Lilburne his for trading in pamphlets, wool or soap. For the doctrine of the talent also taught that all "offices & callings which serve to preserve the good estate of any family, Church or common wealth, are lawfull & of God." Was not every man, since all were equal under the law of God, required to believe "that the calling in which he is; is the particular calling in which God [would] bee served of him"? Any common man needed but to know in his heart that what he did he did sincerely as God's own work, and it followed that what he did was what God would have him do. His own conscience was the judge of his own conduct. "Common actions are as the doer is affected. A sincere man . . . is commanded to serve God in his calling as well as in the Church, and therefore he will not," indeed he cannot, "doe it negligently . . . He will not do it falsely, he will not prophane his calling." Common actions thus performed "with an eye to God" were all "good, and religious actions.

For the Grace of God is a blessed Alcumist, where it toucheth it makes good, and religious."

What was true for men in other occupations was no less but no more true for the preacher, though his task was the harder. He should, said Rogers, follow the rule laid down for every believer, and then he must also follow his special calling, which was to preach. He must have the gift for admonishing, exhorting, comforting and instructing others. He must demonstrate his possession of the gift by securing acknowledgment of its presence in him from those he would serve. He must be able to inspire his hearers to put their own talents to use. His lot was, indeed, not an easy one. Preachers must have more capacious souls than ordinary men since their work was both more difficult and more important, but they had therefore greater trials and temptations to endure.

"Though it must be granted, that they have many more helps in regard of their ministery than private men; yet . . . their troubles and crosses are manie more & greater . . . for they are more shot at by Sathan and his instruments, they have many discouragements, unkindnesses offered them, and hatred for their good will and for doing of their duty."

Such assertions of the special duty and the special danger of preachers in the exercise of their special gift are almost as numerous in the preachers' sermons as the sermons themselves. According to the doctrine of the talent, the only responsibility that could possibly equal theirs was that of the magistrate. These two, in fact, the vocation of the one to preach and of the other to rule, were the poles about which the truly godly state revolved. This principle was presently to be the basic contention of Milton when he took up the argument for Utopia. John Downame presented it much earlier and with admirable clearness. "Princes and Magistrates," he says, perform their services to God "by enacting good

lawes, and seeing them duely executed, making their owne lives (as it were) rules of that obedience which they require of the people, and lively examples and patternes for their imitation." Preachers serve "by leading those which are committed unto their charge, in the waies of truth and godlinesse, not onely by their preaching and writing, instruction, admonition, perswasion and exhortation, but also by practizing those duties which they teach others, and shining before them in the light of a godly life." It will follow, if each has exercised his talent in the fear of the Lord, that the people will also strive to please God, "by yeelding their cheerfull obedience to the godly lawes of Governors, and by imbracing the sound and profitable doctrine, and imitating the Christian and religious examples of their godly Teachers." Thus did the preachers link the doctrine of the talent with their conception of the dual state, one part carnal, the other spiritual, the two complementary. They were, perhaps, dreaming of such a theocracy as indeed they achieved for a time in New England, but they were also, certainly without intention, preparing for a society in which popular education and the free play of public opinion would become the conditions under and by which government must operate.

We have now traced the course of Puritan preaching from its beginning at Cambridge after the expulsion of Cartwright to the time when the spiritual brotherhood had attained a position of power which the rulers of state and church could not let go unchallenged. We have seen how the preachers transposed the teachings of Paul and the doctrine of Calvin into a psychological pattern and a code of behavior for all men to follow. As their work prospered, the godly Utopia again began to dazzle their vision, but before they could reach the New Jerusalem they had to go a long journey and fight many battles.

A Synthesis

ALAN SIMPSON

Alan Simpson (1912–   ) was born in England and came to the United States in 1946. In that year he joined the University of Chicago history department and served there until he became Dean of the College in 1959. In 1964 he left Chicago to become President of Vassar College. Besides his fine work *Puritanism in Old and New England,* from which the following selection is taken, Professor Simpson is the author of numerous articles and *The Wealth of the Gentry, 1540–1660* (1961).

How DOES ONE assess the influence of some profound experience on the subsequent history of a people? The effort of these Puritan saints to seize and dominate the life of English-speaking people in the seventeenth century was obviously such an experience, and everyone who inspects the national consciousness of Englishmen and Americans today finds Puritanism a part of its makeup, whether the inspection is made by ourselves or by strangers who look at us with the incredulity — sometimes kindly, sometimes irritated — of visitors from another world. But what is this Puritanism which has a continuing history? Obviously, it is not the Puritanism which I have been discussing in this book. That is a historical movement with a beginning and an end. It does not repeat itself. Nor is the Puritanism with a continuing history the sum total of the connections which can be traced to Puritanism. Unitarianism can be traced to Puritanism and Transcendentalism to Unitarianism, but is Emerson to be regarded as part of the Puritan tradition? I should say "Yes" only if it could be shown that Emerson was attempting to solve his problems as he believed that Puritans tried to solve theirs or if his solutions bore some direct resemblance to Puritan solutions. Let me foreshorten this type of question and make it more extreme. There were Puritans in the seventeenth century who telescoped into their own lives a history which might take fifty years to work itself out in a dissenting congregation; that is to say, they began as dogmatic Puritans with an intense conviction of their election and ended as lukewarm deists with a few Puritan inhibitions. Is such a man to be considered a Puritan after he has worked his passage from the ages of faith into the ages of reason? I should say not, if the term is to have any meaning at all. Similarly, I should say that the continuing history of Puritanism, if it is to have any useful meaning, must be the continuing history of attempts to solve problems in a Puritan spirit.

To limit it to this is still to leave it sufficiently ambiguous, for it is in the nature of such attempts that they represent selections and adaptations of the original experience. Let me give an example. When the statue of Oliver Cromwell, with his Bible and his sword, which stands in the shadow of the House of Commons, was unveiled toward the close of the last century, the address was given by the Earl of Roseberry. It was a symbolic occasion: the final touch in the adoption of Cromwell as a national hero. After vindicating his essential honesty from all the old charges of ambition and hypocrisy and explaining that the secret of his strength lay in the fact that he

Reprinted from *Puritanism in Old and New England* by Alan Simpson, pp. 99–114, by permission of The University of Chicago Press. Copyright 1955 by The University of Chicago.

38

was a practical mystic, Roseberry continues:

We could find employment for a few Cromwells now. . . . The Cromwell of the nineteenth or the twentieth centuries would not naturally be the Cromwell of the seventeenth. . . . He would not decapitate; he would not rise in revolution or speak the Puritan language. But he would retain his essential qualities as general, as ruler, as statesman. He would be strenuous. He would be sincere. He would not compromise with principles. His faith would be in God and in freedom, and in the influence of Great Britain as promoting both. . . . I know there are some individuals to whom this theory is cant. . . . I know it and I am sorry for them. I believe that the vast majority of our people are inspired by a nobler creed; that their Imperialism, as it is called, is not the lust of dominion or the pride of power, but rather the ideal of Oliver.

Victorian England is making its own appropriation of the Puritan tradition. Puritan itself, it derives strength and purpose from its Puritan past, but it takes what it can use and transforms it in the taking.

Thomas Carlyle might serve as another example. He came from a Calvinist home where he learned the same lessons as the Puritans from the same sacred Book. Like them, he encountered the unbelief and false belief of his generation. He passed through an experience of conversion and discovered his mission in a prophetic ministry. His overpowering sense of divinity, of moral law, of human sin, and of the duty of man to save himself through strenuous self-denial is the same as theirs. He writes their history with an insight into the Puritan soul which few people have ever equaled and trumpets to the modern world that only in deep-hearted believing spirits like Oliver Cromwell will they find the true saviors of society. However, he belongs to no church; he cannot believe that Scripture is literally true; he buries, in what he calls a wise silence, all sorts of questions to which the Puritans had dogmatic answers; and he has enlarged the fraternity of believers to include a pantheon of pagans which would have stupefied his Calvinist ancestors.

But, when all this has been said, the fact remains that the gulf between them is theological rather than moral. If the life of man begins in darkness and ends in darkness, the lesson is to cling all the more passionately to the feeling that there is some kind of order behind the mystery and that this order reveals itself most clearly in the moral sense. And the moral sense to which Carlyle appeals is indestructibly Puritan.

Here, then, is another appropriation of the Puritan tradition. Occasionally the appropriator has some idea of what Puritanism originally stood for and of the kind of selection he is making. No one needed to tell either Roseberry or Carlyle that the Puritan's zeal for freedom was always being overcome by his passion for righteousness and that, if that meant knocking Irish priests over the head or governing Englishmen through major generals, he could do it with a good conscience. Roseberry rejected that side of the Puritan; Carlyle kept it. He was fond of saying that Oliver Cromwell was the best friend poor Ireland ever had. But the appropriator is not usually as familiar with the original Puritans as either Roseberry or Carlyle, and he endows them with all sorts of qualities that they never possessed. However, to say this is only to say that we are dealing with a creative tradition: something which performs its operational function of directing responses to changing situations and which is entitled to bear the original name so long as it shows some correspondence with the original spirit.

If one is looking for the broadest definition of the original Puritanism, it obviously falls into the category of religious revivals. This has been a recurring rhythm in the history of Christian culture, and a more general view than I am taking in these essays would relate Puritanism to earlier revivals. However, if one is to ignore this previous history, and to start with Puritanism, one finds that it has certain drive and that it goes through the typical history of self-discovery, enthusiasm, organization, and decay. It derives its drive from its view of the human predicament. When the Puritan surveys the world within the terms laid down by Christian tradition, he is struck by the profundity of human sin, by the necessity for a work of grace in his own soul to redeem him from the lot of fallen humanity, and by the demand for a disciplined warfare against sin which God makes on those he has saved. His pilgrimage is therefore a search for regeneration, which is usually achieved through an experience of conversion, and for the development of the type of character which is appropriate to the regenerate — a character marked by an intense sense of personal responsibility to God and his moral law, which expresses itself in a strenuous life of self-examination and self-denial. So much for the drive. As for the typical history, it takes rather more than a century to work itself out. The origins of English Puritanism are to be found among the Protestant Reformers of the mid-sixteenth century; it takes shape in the reign of Elizabeth; produces thrust after thrust of energy in the seventeenth century, until the final thrust throws up the Quakers; and then ebbs away.

One contrast lies in the relationship between the Puritan and the intellect of his age. Though I have said in a previous chapter that I think the picture of the Puritan as an intellectual has been overdrawn, to the extent that Puritanism was always more an affair of the heart than of the head, the fact remains that the earlier Puritan did not have to maintain his faith in spite of or against the evidences of philosophy or science. Many Puritans, in my definition, which includes the anti-intellectuals as well as the intellectuals, were neither interested in these evidences nor capable of judging them, but those who were could feel that the truths of Scripture were in harmony with all learning and experience. There was much in the philosophic tradition to support the Puritan. There was little in historical science to shake his faith in Scripture or his conception of human history as the field in which God gathers his elect. There was nothing in the older physical science to cause him great concern: no mechanistic theory of the universe, no displacement of this planet from its central place, no doctrine of evolution. His use of the prophetic books of the Bible to interpret human history, his doctrine of special providences in which God was constantly setting aside the ordinary operations of nature to achieve his purposes, seemed eminently reasonable to him. The result was that among the Puritan scholastics — the last representatives of the medieval ambition to synthesize all experience — it was possible to achieve a fusion of intellect and emotion that was less and less possible for their descendants. Increasingly, it becomes necessary to bury difficult questions in a wise silence or to compromise with them in a way which robs the Puritan impulse of some of its otherworldliness or to shunt them aside. On the whole, evangelism has chosen either to bury or to shunt. Although it has been able to impart its ethical impulse to almost all classes of society, so that even the high aristocrat in Victorian England cultivates a sense of duty and the agnostic himself is a very earnest moralist, it has been less and less able to sound intellectually respectable. And in its extremer forms it becomes a religion of feeling without any intellectual structure at all.

The second contrast lies in the relationship between the Puritan and the religious organization of his society. When the first revival began, his society had a dogmatic religious commitment, and no such thing as toleration existed, apart from the concessions which politicians have always made to expediency. Working within this tradition, the first impulse of the Puritan was to turn his community into a rigorous theocracy. Government of the people, by and for the saints, might be described as his idea of good government. However, partly as a result of divisions among the saints, and of the genuine theory of religious liberty which some saints developed, and partly as the result of developments for which the saints can claim no credit, what emerged from that enterprise was not a theocracy but a regime of toleration. The second revival begins under that regime. In America it is turned into a regime of religious liberty, with the state separated from the church. The diversity of religions left no alternative so far as the federal government was concerned, and the rationalists combined with the evangelicals to get the state churches disestablished. In Britain, religious toleration is turned into a system where no religion is discriminated against, but an established church remains. All this means that the second revival is working within either a liberal or a democratic community. But its theocratic impulse dies hard. The converted soul is likely to cling to its conviction that it has a superior insight into God's design for the social order — a conviction which irritates the unconverted and which is not based on any experience. The belief of Roger Williams that the state should be left to the natural reason which God has bestowed on all his creatures, with the Christian only playing his part as one witness, would seem to be more appropriate. However, if political leaders, like Lincoln, are sometimes afflicted by preachers who insist that God demands the immediate abolition of slavery, these reformers are no longer in a position to use any force but argument.

So much for the obvious contrasts. As for the comparisons, there is the conversion experience, which I have chosen as the central feature of the original Puritanism. There is the fission process, the endless splintering, the Babel of heresies, or the flowering of the sects, whichever you prefer to call it — a process which demonstrates once again how fundamental the individualism of the Protestant Reformation has proved to be compared with its superficial collectivism. There is, furthermore, the same bewildering variety of consequences which the search for regeneration can have; the same variety as it had during the Puritan Revolution. Some ac-

tivities no doubt tend to be shared: an educational mission, a philanthropic mission, a mission to preserve Sabbatarianism or to promote the adoption of Puritan morals, an evangelical impulse which prompts the converted to adopt causes of one description or another. But in this last category it is noticeable that the southern churches feel little disposition to adopt the antislavery cause and that the conversion experience is compatible with every kind of social outlook. John Wesley is a Tory, but the movement he starts will produce liberals, chartists, and socialists. English nonconformity, smarting under the legal privileges and social snobberies of parsons and squires, is either middle or lower class; but English evangelicalism will make as many converts within the privileged classes as outside. Jacksonian democrats like Orestes Brownson are in the tradition of seventeenth-century Levellers, and they are resisted by Puritans in the tradition of seventeenth-century Brahmins. Evangelicalism can mean an individualistic search for salvation or a social gospel. It can reinforce capitalism or produce experiments in communism. It can sustain the privileged or rally the underprivileged. The insights of the converted, as they survey the social scene, are simply not to be marshaled under any single formula.

The final similarity is, of course, in the character. I have said enough in this book about the heroic virtues. The defects have often been made the subject of jibes, and I shall try to restrain myself.

The Puritan has a very limited sense of humor, as one can see from a glance at his portrait. I am thinking not of Grant Wood's "American Gothic" but of seventeenth-century portraits. The corners of the mouths in the divines, at least, are almost invariably pulled down. Emerson has a good phrase for his ancestors. He calls them "the great grim earnest men who solemnized the heyday of their strength by planting New England." I will only add that life seldom struck them as funny. I know that the historian of New England can produce one humorist in Nathaniel Ward; but I have not been so fortunate with the English Puritans. The nearest I came to it was in a Puritan diary, where the author admits he cannot repress his desire to tell a good story, but he tries to keep the account straight by capping every joke with what he calls "a savoury morsel" of divinity. Cromwell's characteristic humor is a sort of horseplay; this is the Cromwell who throws cushions at his officers, who is said to have spattered an officer's face with ink while they were signing the king's death warrant, or who gets a good laugh watching a soldier tip a pail of milk over another soldier's head. Perhaps it is a relief from tension with a touch of hysteria about it; or perhaps it is just the bucolic antics of a plain russet-coated captain. Later in the history of Puritanism a certain humor develops, but it is naturally rather wry — or it has to be indulged when the great Taskmaster is not looking. Of course I do not want to imply that the Puritan, while he is being a Puritan, cannot make a good remark. I have always liked the reply of the revivalist preacher who had not much grammar and was one day ridiculed for it. "That's all right, brother; what little I have I use for the Lord. What do you do with yours?" But you see he is keeping his eye on the main business. Of all the gifts of humor, the only one which blends naturally with the Puritan's purpose is satire: the sort of satire which Carlyle used to such effect in producing conversions.

The other defects of the Puritan character all spring from the fact that he has stripped himself of nonessentials for the struggle and finds it grim. He makes very little contribution to literature outside the didactic sphere. He is likely to regard the arts as the trimmings of life. And he can degenerate into a kill-joy. Macaulay's jibe about the reason why the Puritans suppressed bear-baiting has a grain of symbolic truth in it. They suppressed it, not because it gave pain to the bear, but because it gave pleasure to the spectators.

In conclusion, let us return to the Puritan's impact on politics. Among his virtues I would list:

1. His contribution to our system of limited government. The original Puritans had a genuine basis for their distrust of arbitrary power in addition to their experience of arbitrary government. They thought that man was too sinful to be trusted with too much power. They were likely to make an exception of the saint, but, once saints were prevented from ruling, they have kept their conviction that nobody else should be trusted. The Puritan tradition, with its everlasting insistence that only God is worthy of worship, is one insurance among Anglo-Saxon people that the state has no claim to worship. Fortunately, there are many other securities, but no one will undervalue the stubbornness of this one. They have defended, in season and out of season, the right to preach, to criticize, and to judge. A shrewd observer of the English scene after the Puritan Revolution was struck by the difference it had made to the power of authority to procure respect for its pronouncements:

He [the author] thinketh that the Liberty of the late times gave men so much Light, and diffused it so universally amongst the people, that they are not now to be dealt with, as they might have been in Ages of less enquiry; and therefore tho in some well chosen and dearly beloved Auditories, good resolute Nonsense back'd with Authority may prevail, yet generally Men are become so good Judges of what they hear, that the Clergy ought to be very wary how they go about to impose upon their Understandings, which are grown less humble than they were in former times, when the Men in black had made Learning such a sin in the Laity, that for fear of offending, they made a Conscience of being able to read; but now the World is grown sawcy, and expecteth Reasons, and good ones too, before they give up their own Opinions to other Mens Dictates, tho never so Magisterially deliver'd to them.

2. His contribution to self-government — to the development of initiative and self-reliance in the body of the community.

The Puritan pilgrimage has been a perpetual pilgrimage in self-help. The significance of the dissenting chapel as a training ground for working-class leadership in English history has often been emphasized, and much the same services have been performed by the free church tradition in America. Nor should we forget, in the nineteenth century as in the seventeenth, the direct transfer from church affairs to political affairs of certain techniques of action. The political meeting of the nineteenth century owes an obvious, if not wholly healthy, debt to the camp meeting of the revivalist preacher.

3. His contribution to education. The most anti-intellectual Puritan has been obliged to master at least one book — and that a great one. The most intellectual Puritans, in their desire to promote saving knowledge, have thrown up academy after academy, college after college, until their influence has been writ large over the history of education in England and America.

4. His contribution to morality. The Puritan code has its repellent features, but it is no bad thing to have habits of honesty, sobriety, responsibility, and hard work impressed on a community. It seems probable that the acquisitive energy of the nineteenth century would have created far more havoc than it did without the restraining influence of this evangelical spirit.

Finally, there is the contribution which Puritanism, within the religious tradition of Anglo-Saxon peoples, has made to "the class peace." Almost the worst thing that can happen to the politics of a modern society is to have them polarized around social classes. Any force which works across these divisions, and either conceals or cements them, has a permanent claim on our gratitude.

As the limitations of Puritanism have been sufficiently stressed in these essays, I shall quote only one passage which seems to sum them up. I might have chosen for censure the *cri de coeur* of the nonconformist conscience in nineteenth-century English politics as it appears in the protest of the famous preacher Hugh Price Hughes: "What is morally wrong can never be politically right." Instead, I shall take a passage from an American sermon called "Puritan Principles and the Modern World," which was delivered in 1897:

Puritanism stands for reality; for character; for clean living as a condition of public service; for recognition of responsibility to God; for the supremacy of the spirit. When Oliver Cromwell entered Parliament in 1653, and said, pointing to one member, "There sits a man whose personal conduct is impure and foul"; and then in the name of Almighty God broke up the Parliament, he was the impersonation of Puritanism; and for one, I wish he would rise from his grave and in the same spirit enter some of our halls of legislation, both state and national.

That passage, with its conviction that righteousness ought to prevail, with its tendency to make the Puritan's own moral character a test of political fitness, and with its pressure to turn politics, which ought to be the art of reconciliation, into a moral crusade, reminds us of the darkest blot on his political record.

III. REAPPRAISAL — THE TWENTIETH-CENTURY WATERSHED

The Greatest Englishman of His Age

SAMUEL RAWSON GARDINER

Samuel Rawson Gardiner (1829–1902), one of the most prolific writers and outstanding English historians, was educated at Oxford and early determined to study the history of England during the seventeenth century. The fruits of his work are to be found in his monumental *History of England, 1603–1640*, 14 volumes; *The Great Civil War*, 3 volumes; and *The History of the Commonwealth and Protectorate*, 3 volumes. His work laid the foundation for all intelligent study of the history of England during the first half of that century. What he presents is really a chronicle describing year by year the political and religious history of England. He was always honest and impartial though he never quite succeeded in overcoming his natural leaning toward the Puritan and Parliamentary side. He served as editor of *The English Historical Review* and for twenty-seven years was director of historical publications for the Camden Society. In addition to the above listed works he wrote a *Life of Cromwell* (1899) and *Cromwell's Place in History*, from which the following selection is taken.

FOR THE UNDERSTANDING of Cromwell's character the glimpses afforded by the report of the proceedings of the Army Council in 1647 have a special interest. Only a few accounts of the many discussions in which he took part have been handed down to us, and of those few this is by far the most remarkable. Into the debates of the Council of State after the establishment of the Commonwealth, or of the Council of the Protectorate in later years, scarcely a ray of light has penetrated. The result of our ignorance has been that though Cromwell's moderating influence has been sufficiently revealed in his actions, his long hesitations, his patience in the face of opposition, and his reluctance to break loose from established authority, have been obscured in the popular imagi-nation. In the place of the true image of the man has arisen one of a highhanded despotic ruler, winning his way to power as some think by his force of character, as others think by the unscrupulousness of the means he adopted, but at all events wielding with a heavy hand the power he had gained, and swiftly brushing opposition from his path. The mistake has arisen not from an entire misconception of Cromwell's nature, but from imagining that the character he revealed in special crises was always equally manifested in the daily conduct of his life.

In some sort Cromwell is best understood by fixing his relations to the two great tendencies of the Revolution. In his nature the destructive aims of Puritanism were most clearly revealed. He was intolerant of

From Samuel Rawson Gardiner, *Cromwell's Place in History* (London, 1897), pp. 44–46, 50–52, 102–107, 108–116.

everything opposed to the highest and most spiritual religion, and of the forms which, as he thought, choked and hindered its development. With a strong arm he pronounced a distinct negative to everything persistently antagonistic to what he regarded as the interest of the people of God. After the Battle of Marston Moor he reported with the highest approbation the dying words of one of his officers: "One thing lay on his spirit: that God had not suffered him to be any more the executioner of His enemies." Armed with this faith, Cromwell himself struck blow after blow. He dashed down Laud's mitre and Charles's throne; he was foremost in sending Charles himself to the scaffold; in later years he destroyed Parliament after Parliament. Nor was it merely that his blows were hard. The noticeable thing about them was that they were permanently successful. Never again did there appear in England a persecuting Church supporting itself on royal absolutism; a monarchy resting its claims solely on divine right; a Parliament defying the constituencies by which it had been elected as well as the Government by which it had been summoned. Constitutionalists might challenge the Negative Voice as claimed by Charles to obstruct reform. Cromwell exercised it in right of conformity with the permanent requirements of the nation.

With the other tendency of the times, that towards Parliamentarism, he was certainly not formally in sympathy. He fought for Parliament against the King, not because it was a representative body, but because it was an authority sheltering the principles he championed. He did not, in short, regard it as absolutely essential that a nation should be governed in all times and under all circumstances by a representative assembly. For all that, no man ever appeared more warmly in defence of the two bases on which Parliamentary government can alone prosper: liberty of thought and speech, so far as is consistent with the security of the State, and the committal of the decision in doubtful cases to argument,

thrusting the employment of force as far as possible into the background. If ever there was a man who suffered fools gladly, who sought to influence and persuade, and who was ready to get something tolerable done by consent rather than get something better done by forcing it on unwilling minds, that man was Cromwell.

It is no wonder that Cromwell's success in the battlefield was not followed by permanent political success. In delivering his blows at Marston Moor and Naseby, Cromwell had crushed opposition because he realised all the essential facts of the situation before him, and because he possessed the swiftness of comprehension which enabled him to see — what is seen by few — the relative importance of those facts. His task in dealing with politics was much more difficult. The facts on which his judgment was to be based were far more numerous, and almost infinitely more complicated. In dealing with a people with whose habits of life and thought he was personally familiar, it is, indeed, hardly probable that he would have founded a permanent political system, even if, in the remainder of his career, he had had to address himself merely to the problem of finding a satisfactory government for Englishmen. In any case, however, it was an additional difficulty that he had to consider also the relations between England and the remainder of the British Isles, of whose ways of life he knew little, and the difficulty became still greater when he had to consider the relations between England and the continental states, of whose development and aspirations he knew even less.

In considering the action of Cromwell towards Ireland and Scotland, it will be well to begin by throwing aside the notion that he deliberately sinned against the light. There was, doubtless, ignorance of their past history on his part, and ignorance also of the weakness of force when applied to the solution of political problems; but, on the other hand, it should not be forgotten that statesmen cannot of the very necessity of the case be content with allowing political problems to solve themselves by the action and reaction of natural forces. They have to devise or strengthen some kind of institutions which will afford a shelter to the existing generation for the time being, and give scope for the peaceable development of those forces by which the future is to be moulded.

What, then, did Cromwell accomplish to change the face of history? If we inquire of popular tradition we shall have but little doubt. He won battles; he cut off the King's head; he turned out Parliaments by military compulsion; he massacred the Irish at Drogheda; he made England respected by land and sea.

Is not the popular legend at least roughly in the right? All these things, it will be seen, are negative actions. Hostile armies were not allowed to be victorious; kings were not to be allowed to wield absolute power in disregard of the conditions of the time or the wishes of their subjects; Parliaments were not allowed to disregard public opinion; Irishmen were not allowed to establish a government hostile to England; foreign Powers were not allowed to disregard the force of England. All this is so plain that it needs no further consideration. Our difficulties come in when we ask what was the effect of those constructive efforts which popular tradition passes by. Is tradition right in neglecting these, as it is preeminently right in magnifying the destructive blows dealt with no unstinting hand?

To the student who deals with the details of Cromwell's life a picture very different from that of the popular tradition is apt to present itself. He is compelled to dwell upon the hesitations and the long postponements of action which are no less characteristic of the man than are the swift decisive hammer-strokes which have caught the popular fancy. Yet these two sides of his character have to be harmonised in any complete estimate of the man and his work.

With the man we are here concerned only so far as a knowledge of him may enable us to understand his work, and it is enough to say that there is nothing in the combination of qualities which may fairly be ascribed to Cromwell to render it improbable that he would be as successful in statesmanship as he was in war. If we regard Cromwell's character apart from the circumstances amongst which he moved we should come to the conclusion that it was admirably fitted for the work of directing a State. If large-mindedness, combined with an open eye for facts, together with a shrinking from violence till it seems absolutely necessary to employ it, cannot fit a man to be a statesman, where can we hope to find statesmanship at all? Yet even if we set his management of foreign affairs aside, and restrict ourselves to his dealing with English politics, of which he had far greater personal knowledge, it is impossible to resist the conclusion that he effected nothing in the way of building up where he had pulled down, and that there was no single act of the Protectorate that was not swept away at the Restoration without hope of revival.

It must be remembered that no lasting effects result from any policy, whether negative or positive, which are not in accordance with the permanent tendencies of that portion of the world affected by them. Providence, it is said, is on the side of big battalions. Big battalions, indeed, may do much as far as the immediate future is concerned; but they can do nothing for the distant future. Evesham did not make Edward, when his time came to reign, an absolute sovereign, nor did Falkirk enable him to hand down the undisputed lordship of Scotland to his son. The effect of Naseby, on the other hand, and of the King's execution never were undone. Charles II, indeed, re-ascended the throne, but he sat on it under conditions very different from those of his father, and when James II reverted to his father's conception the Stuart monarchy fell, past recall. So, too, with Cromwell's dealings with the Long Parliament. Never again did England tolerate a Parliament which, being itself but a fragment of its original numbers, set the constituencies at defiance as well as the King.

That Cromwell's success as a destructive force must have stood in the way of his success as a constructive statesman is too obivous to need much labouring, and the proposition is indeed now accepted by all who handle the subject. No man was more aware of the danger than Cromwell himself. He was, at all events, personally disinclined to rattle the sabre to the terror of civilians. It has often been noticed that when Napoleon, before setting out for Waterloo, took the oath to observe the *Acte additionnel,* he appeared in military uniform, and the circumstance has been used to enforce the belief that in heart he was a soldier first and a civilian a long way afterwards. When Cromwell took the oath of the Protectorate, he was clothed in a civilian garb. All his constitutional efforts — efforts for which he had less intellectual aptitude than for any other of the problems he assailed — were directed to the transformation of the Military State into the Civil State. If his attempts were all frustrated, it was because of the impracticability of the task. He was in one sense, as the three Colonels declared, the master of 30,000 men; in another sense, he was their servant. He could not cast them off, as the restored Charles cast them off, because he had no such weight of public sentiment in his favour to support him, to say nothing of the ties by which he was bound to them by common memories and common aspirations. Every day the popular feeling was excited not so much against Cromwell's policy and action, as against his government by military support. How strong was the antagonism aroused appears by the length of time during which fear of military intervention in politics was prolonged. At the Restoration Charles II could only venture to keep up a very small force. In the reign of William III, when the long war came to an end by the Peace of Ryswick, Parliament cut down the army to 10,000 and then to 7,000 men. Even in the time of the younger Pitt an excellent scheme for building barracks was rejected by the House of Commons lest its adoption should, by segregating the soldiers from civilian life, lend itself to their employment against the liberties of civilians.

Revulsion against authority maintained in power by means of the army must therefore be counted as the greatest amongst Cromwell's difficulties. To what extent Puritanism blocked his way it is not so easy to decide. That Puritanism, regarded as an extreme expression of Protestantism and as upholding the rights of the individual conscience against authority, did not perish at the Restoration is beyond all reasonable doubt. It ceased not to find worthy champions to uphold its banner, and by penetrating and informing its conquerors, it became the most precious possession of the nation. Nor is there any convincing reason to suppose that hostility to Puritanism of this kind had much to do with the overthrow of Cromwell's system. The revival of interest in the system of teaching and organisation which had endeared itself to Laud's comrades and disciples was mainly confined, as far as the somewhat scanty evidence in existence reaches, to the Cavalier country gentlemen, and the scholars expelled from the universities, together with those who fell under their influence. There is nothing to show that if the nation at large had been freely consulted on the religious question alone the Restoration would have been accompanied by a violent ecclesiastical reaction, still less that the absence of the ceremonial introduced or restored by Laud was unpopular at any time between the execution of Charles I and the Restoration of Charles II.

In speaking of Puritanism, however, as has been already said, we usually mean something different from this. It implies a system of doctrine and a system of discipline, though prominence was given unequally to these in various parts of the Puritan world. It was in fact a necessity that

Protestantism should be systematised in one way or another. Without discipline, intellectual or physical, it would soon have drifted into anarchy, and into all the weakness that is the inevitable result of anarchy.

. . . The Puritanism of the seventeenth century may fairly be regarded as a backwater, taking its course in a contrary direction to the general current of national development. Like all backwaters the Puritan stream was deflected by an obstacle in its way, the obstacle of Laudian ceremonialism. In the first Parliament of James I the House of Commons had distinctly asserted, "We are no Puritans." In the third Parliament of Charles I it sought to restrain all preachers from declaring anything in opposition to the Calvinistic doctrine. In the Long Parliament the authors of the "Grand Remonstrance" made the most of their determination not "to let loose the golden reins of discipline and government in the Church, or to leave private persons or particular congregations to take up what form of Divine service they please." It was inevitable that when once the fear of Charles and Laud was withdrawn, these pretensions should be somewhat abated. The only question was whether they should be modified from within the Puritan ranks, or battered down from without.

The change so far as it was directed from within was to be directed by Cromwell and by Cromwell's Independent allies. By them the doctrine of religious liberty was preached, and by them was upheld within the limits of practical statesmanship. Cromwell's first task was to preserve liberty of thought, that the "people of God" might be shielded thereby. It was this that made Milton his warm ally, because with Milton liberty was not the negation of restraint, but the condition upon which high design and high achievement depends. Nor was Milton alone in pointing in this direction. It is significant that the one important religious body which originated in the seventeenth century — that of the Society of Friends — owed its strength on the one

hand to that extreme individualism which marks its doctrine as the quintessence of the higher Puritanism, but on the other hand to its unshrinking opposition to the Calvinistic discipline and the Calvinistic doctrine. No wonder Cromwell was drawn to its founder. "If thou and I," said the Protector, "were but an hour of the day together, we should be nearer one to the other."

Yet it was not Cromwell who founded religious liberty in England. His system perished at the Restoration, and when the idea was revived under the guise of toleration it came from another quarter altogether. It was not from Puritanism, high or low, that the gift was received, but from the sons of those Cavaliers and Presbyterians who had been Cromwell's bitterest enemies.

What, then, was the secret of Cromwell's failure to establish — not his dynasty, for that is of little importance — but his ideas? First, amongst the causes of failure must be reckoned his dependence on the army. The master of 30,000, or rather of 57,000, men could not win over a spirited nation which abhorred the rule of the soldiery, however veiled, and no less abhorred the taxation necessary for their support. It was all the more difficult to reconcile the nation and the army because that army had not won its renown in combat with an alien foe. Unlike the soldiers of Napoleon, the men of the New Model had no Marengos or Jenas to boast of, victories which went to the heart of the French citizen as well as of the French soldier. Their laurels had been gathered in civil wars, and whilst the conquered ascribed to them the diminution of their estates, those who had formerly applauded the conquerors forgot their services in their more recent pretensions. Cromwell, who could not dispense with the army, was pushed on to give it popularity by launching it against foreign nations. It was all in vain. Englishmen refused to regard that army with pride and enthusiasm, as their descendants regarded the army that struck down Napoleon a

Waterloo, or that died at its post before the beleaguered fortress of Sebastopol.

Indirectly, too, the military rule which Cromwell was never able to shake off endangered the permanence of his system, and must have endangered it even if, as his unreasoning worshippers fondly urge, his span of life had been prolonged for twenty years. It is the condition on which all strong intellectual and spiritual movements rest that they shall be spontaneous. They win their way by force of inward conviction, not by the authority of the State. How earnestly Cromwell desired to set conviction before force is known to all. He had broken the Presbyterian and Calvinistic chains, and had declared his readiness to see Mohammedanism professed in England rather than that the least of the saints of God should suffer wrong. Yet he dared not give equal liberty to all. To the Royalists his person was hateful alike as the murderer of the King, as the General whose army had despoiled them of their property, and as the violator of "the known laws" of the land. How, then, could he tolerate the religion of the Book of Common Prayer, which had become the badge of Royalism? It is true that the tide of persecution rose and fell, and that it was never very violent even at its worst; but it is also true that it could never be disowned. There was to be complete freedom for those who were Puritans, little or none for those who were not. Liberty of religion was to be co-extensive with the safety of the State. It was a useful formula, but hardly more when the safety of the State meant the predominance of an army, and the head of the State dared not throw himself on a free Parliament to give him a new basis of authority.

Nor was Puritanism itself, even after it had been cleansed in the waters of liberty, fitted to hold the directing power in the State. Though the checks which it placed upon worldly amusements have been over-estimated, it certainly did not regard such amusements with favour. Like all great spiritual movements, it was too strenuous, too self-contained to avoid drawing the reins over-tightly on the worldling. All that was noblest in it would be of better service when it was relegated from the exercise of power to the employment of influence.

What, then, is Cromwell's place in history? If we regard the course of the two centuries which followed his death, it looks as if all that need be said might be summed up in a few words. His negative work lasted, his positive work vanished away. His constitutions perished with him, his Puritanism descended from the proud position to which he had raised it, his peace with the Dutch Republic was followed by two wars with the United Provinces, his alliance with the French monarchy only led to a succession of wars with France lasting into the nineteenth century. All that endured was the support given by him to maritime enterprise, and in that he followed the tradition of the Governments preceding him.

Yet, after all, the further we are removed from the days in which Cromwell lived, the more loth are we to fix our eyes exclusively on that part of his work which was followed by immediate results. It may freely be admitted that his efforts to establish the national life upon a new basis came to nothing, without thinking any the worse of the man for making the attempt. It is beginning to be realised that many, if not all, the experiments of the Commonwealth were but premature anticipations of the legislation of the nineteenth century, and it is also beginning to be realised that, whatever may be our opinion of some of Cromwell's isolated actions, he stands forth as the typical Englishman of the modern world. That he will ever be more than this is not to be expected. Even if Scotchmen forget the memories of Dunbar and Worcester, it is certain that Drogheda and Wexford will not pass out of the minds of Irishmen. It is in England that his fame has grown up since the publication of Carlyle's monumental work, and it is as an Englishman that he must be judged.

What may be fairly demanded alike of

Cromwell's admirers and of his critics is that they shall fix their eyes upon him as a whole. To one of them he is the champion of liberty and peaceful progress, to another the forcible crusher of free institutions, to a third the defender of oppressed peoples, to a fourth the asserter of his country's right to dominion. Every one of the interpreters has something on which to base his conclusions. All the incongruities of human nature are to be traced somewhere or other in Cromwell's career. What is more remarkable is that this union of apparently contradictory forces is precisely that which is to be found in the English people, and which has made England what she is at the present day.

Many of us think it strange that the conduct of our nation should often appear to foreign observers in colours so different from those in which we see ourselves. By those who stand aloof from us we are represented as grasping at wealth and territory, incapable of imaginative sympathy with subject races, and decking our misconduct with moral sentiments intended to impose on the world. From our own point of view, the extension of our rule is a benefit to the world, and subject races have gained far more than they have lost by submission to a just and beneficent administration, whilst our counsels have always, or almost always, been given with a view to free the oppressed and to put a bridle in the mouth of the oppressor.

That both these views have truth in them no serious student of the present and the past can reasonably deny. Whatever we may say, we are and have been a forceful nation, full of vigorous vitality, claiming empire as our due, often with scant consideration for the feelings and desire of other peoples. Whatever foreigners may say, we are prone, without afterthought, to place our strength at the service of morality and even to feel unhappy if we cannot convince ourselves that the progress of the human race is forwarded by our action. When we enter into possession, those who look on us from the outside dwell upon the irregularity of our conduct in forcing ourselves into possession; whilst we, on the contrary, dwell upon the justice and order maintained after we have once established ourselves.

With Cromwell's memory it has fared as with ourselves. Royalists painted him as a devil. Carlyle painted him as the masterful saint who suited his peculiar Valhalla. It is time for us to regard him as he really was, with all his physical and moral audacity, with all his tenderness and spiritual yearnings, in the world of action what Shakespeare was in the world of thought, the greatest because the most typical Englishman of all time. This, in the most enduring sense, is Cromwell's place in history. He stands there, not to be implicitly followed as a model, but to hold up a mirror to ourselves, wherein we may see alike our weakness and our strength.

A Rare and Noble Leader

CHARLES H. FIRTH

Sir Charles Firth (1857–1936) did his work at Oxford, and, in 1883 settled there for the remainder of his life. Tremendously influenced by S. R. Gardiner he became especially interested in seventeenth-century history. Sir Charles
carried on Gardiner's writing from the year 1656 to 1658 and intended to go
to the Restoration, but the plans were never carried out. One of the founders
of the *English Historical Review,* Sir Charles also was a prolific contributor to
the *Dictionary of National Biography,* for which he wrote more than 225 lives.
He served as president of the Royal Historical Society from 1913 to 1917 and
also as a member of the Historical Manuscripts Commission. He wrote books and
articles, edited documents, and was most generous with his advice and encouragement to other writers. Knighthood was conferred upon him in 1922.

CROMWELL came into power as the nominee of the army, and in do-
mestic affairs the programme which he set himself to carry out was that which the army had set forth in its petitions and manifestoes. For the moment he was invested with all the authority of a dictator. According to the "Instrument of Govern-
ment," the first triennial Parliament was to meet in September, 1654, and in the inter-
val the Protector and his Council were em-
powered to issue ordinances, which had the force of law "until order shall be taken in Parliament concerning them." Cromwell made a liberal use of this provision, and the period of nine months which followed his accession was the creative period of his government. Between December, 1653, and September, 1654, he issued eighty-two or-
dinances, nearly all of which were con-
firmed in 1656 by his second Parliament. Hallam, in a disparaging comparison be-
tween Cromwell and Napoleon, concludes by saying that Cromwell, unlike Napoleon, "never showed any signs of a legislative mind, or any desire to fix his renown on that noblest basis, the amelioration of social institutions." In reality, nothing could be farther from the truth, and if Cromwell's reforming zeal has left no trace on the statute book, the reason is that all the laws passed during the Protectorate were an-
nulled at the Restoration.

All the leading principles of Cromwell's domestic policy are contained in the small folio volume of his ordinances. A few are merely prolongations of expiring acts, others are personal or local in their application. There is an ordinance for the relief of poor prisoners, another codifying the law relat-
ing to the maintenance of highways, and there are three devoted to the reorganisation of the Treasury. The settlement of Ireland and Scotland, and the completion of the union of the three kingdoms, which the Long Parliament had left unfinished, form the subject of a third series. But none ex-
hibit so plainly the Protector's domestic pol-
icy as the three sets of ordinances dealing with the reform of the Law, the reformation of manners, and the reorganisation of the national Church.

Ever since 1647, the army had demanded that the laws of England should be so re-
formed, "that all suits and questions of right may be made more clear and certain in their issues, and not so tedious nor chargeable in their proceedings." The Long

From Charles H. Firth, *Oliver Cromwell and the Rule of the Puritans in England* (London, 1938), pp. 346–369. Reprinted by permission of G. P. Putnam's Sons, New York, and Oxford University Press, London.

Parliament took the task in hand, made some slight progress, and then stuck fast. The Little Parliament attempted it with so much rude vigour that it seemed likely to end in the subversion of all law. The Protector took up the work where the Long Parliament left off, and persistently pursued it as long as he ruled.

Cromwell realised its difficulty. "If any man," he once said, "should ask me, 'Why, how will you have it done?' I confess I do not know." All he could do was to select the best men for the purposes, and to leave them a free hand. Therefore he applied to the lawyers to co-operate, "being resolved to give the learned of the robe the honour of reforming their profession," and hoping "that God will give them hearts to do it." His chief assistant was Matthew Hale, who was made a judge by the Protector early in 1654. At the opening of Parliament in September, 1654, Cromwell announced that the Government had called together "persons of as great ability and great interest as are in the nation, to consider how the laws might be made plain and short, and less chargeable to the people," and that they had prepared several bills. The most important of these schemes was the ordinance for the regulation of the Court of Chancery, published August 21, 1654, and confirmed by Parliament in 1656. It contained a reduced scale of fees, and embodied, according to modern lawyers, many valuable reforms. Contemporary practitioners, such as Whitelocke, held that there was much in the new procedure which it was impossible or undesirable to carry out, but with some subsequent modifications it was duly put in force.

Cromwell was equally zealous for the reform of the Criminal Law. In April, 1653, as soon as he had turned out the Long Parliament, he gave pardons to all prisoners sentenced to death except those guilty of murder. His object was to make the laws "conformable to the just and righteous laws of God." Some English laws, he told Parliament, were "wicked and abominable laws."

"To hang a man for six and eightpence and I know not what — to hang for a trifle and acquit murder, is in the ministration of the law through ill framing of it. . . . To see men lose their lives for petty matters is a thing God will reckon, and I wish it may not be laid on this nation a day longer than you have opportunity to give a remedy."

To carry out these schemes required not merely the help of lawyers to devise them, but the co-operation of Parliament to make them law. The Protector's first Parliament spent all its time in consitutional debates, and did nothing to reform the Law. His second, busy most of its existence in the like manner, discussed the bills introduced by the Government for the establishment of county registers and local courts, but allowed them to drop. It completed the abolition of feudal incidents which the Long Parliament had commenced, and which Charles II's Parliament finally placed on the statute book, but it left the harshness and cruelty of the criminal code for the nineteenth century to redress.

The "Reformation of Manners" was an object in which the Protector obtained more support from Parliament. All Puritans were eager for it, and the Long Parliament had made a beginning by acts enjoining the stricter observance of Sunday, punishing swearing with greater severity, and making adultery a capital offence. Of the Protector's ordinances, one declared duelling "unpleasing to God, unbecoming Christians, and contrary to all good order and government." A person sending a challenge was to be bound over to keep the peace for six months, and a duellist who killed his opponent was to be tried for murder. A second ordinance supplemented the act against swearing by special provisions for the punishment of carmen, porters, and watermen, "who are very ordinarily drunk and do blaspheme." A third forbade cockfighting, because it often led to disturbances of the peace and was accompanied by gaming and drunkenness. A fourth suppressed horse-racing for six months, not because of its accompaniments, but because the Cavaliers made use of race-meetings "to carry on their pernicious designs."

When Cromwell's second Parliament met, he appealed to it to further the work. . . .

Parliament answered by confirming the ordinances against duelling, swearing, and cock-fighting, and passing similar acts of its own. One was directed against the vagrants and "idle, dissolute" persons who abounded in all parts of the country. Amongst them, "the bigots of that iron time" included fiddlers and minstrels taken "playing or making music" in taverns, who were declared punishable as "rogues and vagabonds." A second act was aimed at the professional gamesters about London, who made it their trade "to cheat and debauch the young gentry." A third act enforced the Puritan Sabbath in all its severity. On that day, no shops might be opened and no manufactures carried on. No travelling was to be allowed, except in cases of necessity attested by a certificate from a justice, and persons "vainly and profanely walking on the day aforesaid" were to be punished. Sunday closing was the rule for all inns and alehouses, though the dressing or sale of victuals in a moderate way, "for the use of such as cannot otherwise be provided for," was permitted.

Much of this drastic legislation was ineffective. In some cases it went far beyond the feeling of the times. Juries steadily refused to convict persons charged with adultery under the act of 1650, and it is doubtful whether the capital penalty was ever actually inflicted. In many places, the local authorities were indifferent or timid. "We may have good laws," said the Protector, "against the common country disorders that are everywhere, yet who is to execute them?" Hardly the country justices. "A justice of the peace shall by most be wondered at as an owl, if he go but one step out of the ordinary course of his fellow justices in the reformation of these things." Hence the value in Cromwell's eyes of the Major-Generals established throughout England in the autumn of 1655. They were not simply military officers charged to keep an eye on the political enemies of the government, but police magistrates required to repress crime and immorality in their respective districts. Pride put a stop to bear-baiting in London by killing the bears, and to cock-fighting by wringing the necks of the cocks. Whalley boasted, after he had been a few months in office, that there were no vagrants left in Nottinghamshire, and in every county his colleagues suppressed unnecessary alehouses by the score. Nor was it only humble offenders who were struck at: neither the rich nor the noble escaped the impartial severity of these military reformers. "Let them be who they may that are debauched," said Cromwell, "it is for the glory of God that nothing of outward consideration should save them from a just punishment and reformation." He claimed that the establishment of the Major-Generals had been "more effectual towards the discountenancing of vice and the settling of religion than anything done these fifty years." Their rule ended in the spring of 1657, and Cromwell feared that the work of reformation would come to a stop. But the experiment had infused new vigour into the local administration, which lasted as long as the Protectorate endured.

In spite of these restrictive laws, it must not be imagined that there was any general suppression of public amusements or sports. "Lawful and laudable recreations" even Puritans encouraged. In 1647, when the Long Parliament prohibited the observation of Christmas and of saints' days in general, it passed an act giving servants, apprentices, and scholars a whole holiday once a month, for "recreation and relaxation from their constant and ordinary labours." The Protector himself hunted, hawked, and played bowls, just as if he had been a Royalist country-gentleman. He told Parliament that he suppressed race-meetings not because they were unlawful, but because they were temporarily inexpedient. With all his zeal for Sunday closing, the suppression of unnecessary alehouses, and the punishment of drunkenness, it never occurred to him to stop the sale of drink altogether. He drank wine and small beer himself, and quoted as illogical and absurd "the man who would keep all wine out of the country lest men should be drunk." The idea was contrary to his conception of civil freedom. "It will be found," he said, "an unjust and unwise jealousy to deprive a man of his natural liberty upon a supposition he may abuse it. When he doth abuse it, judge."

In the moral crusade he had undertaken, the Protector relied not so much on restrictive legislation as on the influence of education and religion. It was to their defective education that he attributed much of the misconduct of the "profane nobility and gentry of this nation." "We send our children to France," he said, "before they know God or good manners, and they return with all the licentiousness of that nation. Neither is care taken to educate them before they go, or to keep them in good order when they come home." As a party, the Puritans showed a great zeal for education, and the pamphlet literature of the time is full of schemes for its reformation or extension. In these discussions, the modern conception of the duty of the State with regard to education gradually took shape. While the plan of education which Milton published in 1644 was intended only for "a select body of our noble and gentle youth," in 1660, he advocated the foundation of schools in all parts of the nation, in order to spread knowledge, civility, and culture to "all extreme parts which now lie numb and neglected." In his Oceana, Harrington asserted that the formation of future citizens by means of a system of free schools was one of the chief duties of a republic.

As usually happens, practical men lagged behind the theorists, but during the Commonwealth a portion of the revenue of confiscated Church lands was systematically devoted to the maintenance of schools and schoolmasters. The Protector pursued the same policy, and publicly declared when appropriating a grant for educational pur-

poses in Scotland, that it was "a duty not only to have the Gospel set up, but schools for children erected and maintenance provided therefor." His government undertook the task of ejecting incapable schoolmasters and of licensing persons fit to teach. It made the proper administration of educational endowments in general a part of its business, and one of Cromwell's earliest ordinances appointed fresh commissioners for the visitation of the universities, and established a permanent board of visitors for the great public schools. Personally, he was far more interested in the reorganisation of the universities than in primary or secondary education. He vigorously defended them against the attacks of the zealots of the Little Parliament who threatened their disendowment or abolition. In 1651, he had been elected Chancellor of Oxford, and held that office till July, 1657, when he was succeeded by his son Richard, signalising his connection with the university by the foundation of a new readership in Divinity, and the presentation of some Greek manuscripts to the Bodleian. He appointed John Owen his Vice-Chancellor, under whose efficient rule Oxford prospered greatly. Even Clarendon is forced to admit that in spite of visitations and purgings the university "yielded a harvest of extraordinary good and sound knowledge in all parts of learning."

The Protector also endeavoured to found a new university in the north of England. There was a widespread feeling that the two existing universities were not enough for the country. In 1641, petitions were presented praying for the foundation of a university at York or Manchester, and later it was proposed to establish one in London. In 1651, Cromwell strongly recommended the endowment of a school or college for all the sciences and literature, out of the property of the Dean and Chapter of Durham. The scheme, he wrote, was "a matter of great concernment and importance, at that which by the blessing of God may conduce to the promoting of learning and piety in these poor, rude, ignorant parts," and bring forth in time "such happy and glorious fruits as are scarce thought of or foreseen." But Parliament did nothing, and it was reserved for Oliver himself to found a college at Durham in 1657, which throve greatly until the Restoration put an end to its existence.

The Protector encouraged learned men and men of letters. With his relative, the poet Waller, he was on terms of considerable intimacy; he allowed Hobbes and Cowley, both Royalists, to return from exile, and he released Cleveland when he was arrested by one of the Major-Generals, although Cleveland's fame rested mainly on satires against the Puritans. Milton and Marvell were in Cromwell's service as Latin secretaries, and he also employed Marvell as tutor to one of his wards. Brian Walton was assisted in the printing of his Polyglot Bible, and Archbishop Ussher was honoured by a public funeral.

But both learning and education were, in Cromwell's eyes, inseparably connected with religion. When he accepted the Chancellorship he congratulated Oxford on the learning and piety "so marvellously springing up there," adding a hope that it might be "useful to that great and glorious kingdom of our Lord Jesus Christ." Thinking that the chief function of the universities was to provide ministers for the Church, he held piety more important than learning. "I believe," he told his Parliament, five years later, "that God hath for the ministry a very great seed in the youth of the universities, who, instead of studying books, study their own heart." Cromwell's desire to develop higher education, and his defence of the universities against their assailants, were the natural consequences of his resolve to maintain a national Church against those who wished to sever the connection between Church and State. On this question, the army, as a whole, supported Cromwell. In the "Agreement of the People," presented to Parliament in 1649, the army had demanded that "the Christian religion be held forth and recommended as the public profession of this nation," and it included "the instructing of the people thereunto, so it be not compulsive," and "the maintaining able teachers for that end," amongst the legitimate functions of the government. These principles had been embodied in the "Instrument of Government," and the duty of devising means to carry them out fell to the Protector.

The first question to be decided was the question of the maintenance of the clergy. The Little Parliament had proposed to abolish tithes altogether, and in the "Instrument of Government" the substitution of some other provision was suggested. As no satisfactory scheme for the commutation of tithes could be devised, Cromwell felt bound to preserve them. "For my part," said he, "I should think I were very treacherous if I took away tithes till I see the legislative power settle maintenance to ministers another way." To abolish tithes before that was done, would be "to cut the throats of the ministers." Under the Protectorate, as under the rule of the Long Parliament, it was the permanent policy of the government to increase the income of the parochial clergy. The endowments of poor livings were systematically augmented out of the fund supplied by episcopal lands and the fines imposed on royalist delinquents.

The basis of the Protector's plan for the reorganisation of the Church was the scheme which John Owen had presented to the Long Parliament in 1652. On March 20, 1654, Cromwell issued an ordinance "for the approbation of public preachers," which appointed thirty-eight commissioners, lay and clerical, to sit permanently in London and examine into the qualifications of all candidates for livings. Their business was to certify that they found the candidate "to be a person for the grace of God in him, his holy and unblamable conversation, as also for his knowledge and utterance, able and fit to preach the Gospel," and without obtaining this certificate no one was in future to be admitted to a benefice. The commissioners were not empowered to impose any doctrinal tests, and it was expressly declared that approbation by them "is not intended nor shall be construed to be any solemn or sacred setting apart of any person to any particular office in the ministry." All that the "Triers" undertook to do was to see that none but fit and proper persons should receive "the public stipend and maintenance" guaranteed by the State.

After provision for the appointment of the fit, came provision for the elimination of the unfit. A second ordinance, issued in August, 1654, appointed local commissioners in every county to remove scandalous and inefficient ministers and schoolmasters within its limits. Amongst the reasons which justified ejection were included not merely immoral conduct or Popish and blasphemous opinions, but disaffection to the government and the use of the Prayer-book. In September, the work was completed by a third ordinance for the union of small and the division of large and populous parishes.

Cromwell's speeches are full of expressions of satisfaction at the results that these ordinances produced. He was proud of the character of his clergy. "In the time of Episcopacy," said he, "what pitiful certificates served to make a man a minister. If any man understood Latin or Greek, he was sure to be admitted." But now, "neither Mr. parson nor doctor in the university hath been reckoned stamp enough by those that made these approbations, though I can say they have a great esteem for learning." The rule with the Triers was, "that they must not admit a man unless they were able to discern something of the grace of God in him."

He was equally proud of the comprehensiveness of the Church. There were "three sorts of godly men," that is, three sects, to be provided for in it: the Presbyterians, the Independents, and the Baptists. The Triers were drawn impartially from all three bodies, and "though a man be of any of those three judgments, if he have the root of the matter in him he may be admitted." Summing up the work of the Triers and Ejectors, he emphatically declared: "There

hath not been such a service to England since the Christian religion was perfect in England."

In the main, Cromwell's satisfaction was justified. Both bodies of commissioners did the work they were charged to do with fidelity. Some good men were expelled merely for royalism or using the liturgy, but the bulk of those who lost their livings deserved their fate, and those admitted were generally fit for their office.

Outside the bounds of the national Church, the constitution promised liberty of worship to "all such as do profess faith in God by Jesus Christ." Anglicanism and Catholicism, however, labelled Prelacy and Popery, and regarded as idolatrous or politically dangerous, were excepted by name from this promise. In practice, although the use of the liturgy had been prohibited since 1645, many orthodox Anglicans had contrived to retain their livings, sometimes using portions of the Prayer-book from memory, in other cases confining themselves to preaching and to the administration of the sacraments. Many ejected ministers gathered little congregations in private houses, and were not molested by the Government. The royalist insurrection of 1655 led to greater severity, and in October, 1655, Cromwell issued a proclamation prohibiting the employment of the ejected clergy as chaplains or schoolmasters. It was meant as a warning, rather than to be rigidly enforced, and the promise was made that any man whose "godliness and good affection to the present government" were capable of proof should be treated with tenderness. Congregations of Royalists continued to meet in London throughout the Protectorate, and the Government winked at their use of Anglican services and ceremonies. But whenever there was a new plot discovered, their meetings were liable to be interrupted by the soldiery.

The case of the Catholics was harder than that of the Anglicans, although their lot was less hard than it had been. In 1650, the acts imposing fines on recusants for not coming to church were repealed, and there vere persistent rumours that the Independents were about to make proposals for their oleration. In June, 1654, a Catholic priest was executed in London for no crime except being a priest. Cromwell, it is said, wished to pardon him but was prevented by the opposition of his Council. In 1656, Mazarin urged Cromwell to grant toleration to the Catholics.

"I cannot," answered the Protector,

s to a public declaration of my sense on that oint; although I believe that under my government your Eminency on behalf of the Catholics has less cause for complaint than nder the Parliament. For I have of some and nose very many had compassion, making a ifference. I have plucked many out of the re, — the raging fire of persecution, which id tyrannise over their consciences and encroach by arbitrariness of power over their states. And herein it is my purpose, as soon s I can remove impediments and some weights that press me down, to make a further progress, and discharge my promise to our Eminence.

The Protector's purpose was never fulfilled. Public opinion in England was too hostile o the Catholics to permit of their legal oleration, and the same thing happened when Cromwell wished to readmit the Jews o England. In November, 1655, Manasseh Ben Israel, a learned Portuguese Jew, settled in Amsterdam as a physician, petitioned the Protector to allow the Jews to eside and trade in England, and to grant hem the free exercise of their religion. Cromwell, who was personally in favour f this petition, called together a committee of divines, merchants, and lawyers to onfer with the Council on the question. The Protector himself took part in the conferences. "I never heard a man speak so well," said one of his hearers, but the divines feared for the religion and the merchants for their trade, so the legal toleration he Jews asked for was not granted. Cromwell, however, granted them leave to meet n private houses for devotion, and showed hem such encouragement and favour that

their resettlement in England really dates from the Protectorate.

The Protector's tolerant nature showed itself again in his dealings with the Quakers. Under the Commonwealth, the Quakers were persecuted and imprisoned, not simply because their opinions were regarded as blasphemous, but because they were held dangerous to the public peace. Their attacks on the clergy and their misconduct and brawling in churches gave colour to these accusations. Under the Protectorate, this persecution continued, till it was mitigated by the intervention of the Protector and his Council. In 1654, George Fox had a long interview with the Protector. "I spake much to him," writes Fox, "of truth; and a great discourse I had with him about religion, wherein he carried himself very moderately." The earnestness and enthusiasm of Fox impressed Cromwell greatly.

As I spake, he would several times say, it was very good, and it was truth. And as I was turning to go away, he catches me by the hand, and with tears in his eyes, said: "Come again to my house; for if thou and I were but an hour of a day together we should be nearer one to the other"; adding, that he wished me no more ill than he did to his own soul.

Convinced that the Quakers were not inclined to "take up a carnal sword" against his government, the Protector ordered Fox to be set free, and in October, 1656, he released a number of imprisoned Quakers. Again in November, 1657, he issued a general circular to all justices in England and Wales, stating that though he was far from countenancing the mistaken practices or principles of the Quakers, yet as those proceeded "rather from a spirit of error than a malicious opposition to authority," they were "to be pitied, and dealt with as persons under a strong delusion," to be discharged from prison, and to be treated in the future with tenderness rather than severity.

Yet tolerant as Cromwell was, there were limits to his toleration, and certain opinions he regarded as outside the pale. The Instrument refused liberty to "such as under the profession of Christ hold forth and practise licentiousness."

A well-ordered state, thought Cromwell, should in this respect resemble an army, but, even with regard to opinions which he held blasphemous, he was not willing to suffer the extreme penalties to be inflicted which the law sanctioned and the voice of most Puritans demanded.

In 1656, James Naylor, an old soldier who was one of Fox's early disciples, allowed himself to be hailed by his enthusiastic followers as a new Messiah, and was consequently thrown into prison as a blasphemer. The Parliament then sitting assumed judicial powers, and, after many days' debate voted that he should be branded, pilloried, whipped, and imprisoned at pleasure. The Protector vainly pointed out to the House that it was going beyond its powers, and all the influence of the Government was required to save Naylor from capital punishment. What the Protector would probably have done if the punishment of Naylor had been left to him was shown by his treatment of John Biddle. Unitarians were by implication excluded from toleration by the Petition and Advice. In 1655, Biddle was prosecuted under the Blasphemy Act of 1648, and would undoubtedly have been sentenced to death. The Protector was petitioned to interfere, and replied by soundly rating the petitioners. "If it be true," said he, "what Mr. Biddle holds, to wit, that our Lord and Saviour Jesus Christ is but a creature, then all those who worship Him with the worship due to God are idolaters." No Christian, was his conclusion, could give any countenance to such a person, but nevertheless he stopped the trial by issuing a warrant for Biddle's confinement at St. Mary's Castle in the Scilly Islands. Biddle's life was undoubtedly saved by this intervention.

In spite of the liberality and comprehensiveness of Cromwell's ecclesiastical policy, there were several sections of Puritans whom it failed to satisfy. Some Independ-

ents opposed any established Church, and denied that the State ought in any way to meddle with religious matters. The most distinguished adherents of this view were Vane and Milton. The magistrate, said Milton, had coercive power in all matters of religion. It was not his business "to settle religion," as it was popularly termed, "by appointing either what we shall believe in divine things or practise in religious." His duty was simply to defend the Church. "Had he once learned not further to concern himself with Church affairs, half his labour might be spared and the Commonwealth better tended."

Another section, in the name of liberty of conscience, denied the State any right to punish blasphemous or immoral doctrines. "They tell the Magistrate," said the Protector, "that he hath nothing to do with men holding such notions; these are matters of conscience and opinion; they are matters of religion; what hath the Magistrate to do with these things? He is to look to the outward man, not to the inward." Cromwell's own position with regard to dangerous opinions was that, if they were but opinions, they were best left alone. "Notions will hurt none but those that have them." When they developed into actions, it was a different matter, and especially when they led to rebellion and bloodshed. "Our practice hath been," he said in 1656, "to let all this nation see that whatever pretensions to religion would continue quiet and peaceable, they should enjoy conscience and liberty to themselves." But to be quiet and peaceable was the indispensable condition. Fifth Monarchy preachers were frequently arrested for sermons against the government, both before and after the attempted rising of the Fifth Monarchy men in the spring of 1657. On one occasion, some of the congregation of John Rogers, one of their preachers, came to Whitehall to argue with the Protector, complaining that their pastor was suffering for religion's sake. Cromwell answered that Rogers suffered as a railer, a seducer, and a stirrer-up of sedition: that to call suffering for evil-doing suffering for the Gospel was to make Christ the patron of such things. "God is my witness," he concluded,

no man in England doth suffer for the testimony of Jesus. Nay, do not lift up your hands and your eyes, for there is no man in England which suffers so. There is such liberty — I wish it be not abused, that no man in England suffereth for Christ.

It was true. Cromwell's was the most tolerant government which had existed in England since the Reformation. In practice, he was more lenient than the laws, and more liberal-minded than most of his advisers. The drawback was, that even the more limited amount of religious freedom which the laws guaranteed seemed too much to the great majority of the nation. Englishmen — even Puritans — had not yet learnt the lesson of toleration. "Is there not yet," said Cromwell in 1655, "a strange itch upon the spirits of men? Nothing will satisfy them unless they can press their finger upon their brethren's consciences to pinch them there."

To induce these jarring sects to co-operate was more difficult, but that also Cromwell attempted to do. In the Puritan Church, which he organised, no agreement about ritual or discipline or doctrine was required, save only the acceptance of the main principles of Christianity. It was not so much a Church as a confederation of Christian sects working together for righteousness, under the control of the State. The absence of agreement in details and of uniformity in externals was no defect in Cromwell's eyes. To him it was rather a merit. "All that believe," he had once written, "have the real unity which is more glorious because inward and spiritual."

The originality of the Protector's ecclesiastical policy lay in this attempt to combine the two principles of toleration and comprehension. It reflected his character. His tolerance was not the result of scepticism or indifference, but arose from respect for the consciences of others. The comprehensiveness of his Church was the outcome of his large-hearted sympathy with every form of Puritanism. To local magistrates in local religious quarrels, he enjoined "a charity as large as the whole flock of Christ"; and the same spirit inspired his exhortation to the Little Parliament.

Have a care of the whole flock. Love the sheep. Love the lambs. Love all; cherish and countenance all in all things that are good. And if the poorest Christian, the most mistaken Christian, shall desire to live peaceably and quietly under you: I say if any desire but to live a life of godliness and honesty, let him be protected.

Mr. Greatheart, under whose protection all pilgrims to the Celestial City walked securely — Feeble-Mind and Ready-to-Halt, as well as Valiant-for-Truth — is but an allegorical representation of what Cromwell was to the Puritans. Cromwell's ecclesiastical system passed away with its author, but no man exerted more influence on the religious development of England. Thanks to him, Nonconformity had time to take root and to grow so strong in England that the storm which followed the Restoration had no power to root it up. . . .

The Puritan Spirit

R. H. TAWNEY

One of the leading economic historians and prominent writers on socialism, Richard H. Tawney (1880–1962) here discusses religion and the rise of capitalism. After teaching at Glasgow and Oxford Universities, he occupied the chair of Economic History at the London School of Economics for many years. Although a leading member of the British Labour Party since its early years he wrote many articles and books which were critical of that party. Four years before his death he produced a masterful work, *Business and Politics under James I: Lionel Cranfield as Merchant and Minister,* which stimulated quite a controversy. The following selection taken from his most famous and controversial work was based on lectures given in 1922.

THE CAPITALIST SPIRIT" is as old as history, and was not, as has sometimes been said, the offspring of Puritanism. But it found in certain aspects of later Puritanism a tonic which braced its energies and fortified its already vigorous temper. At first sight, no contrast could be more violent than that between the iron collectivism, the almost military discipline, the remorseless and violent rigors practiced in Calvin's Geneva, and preached elsewhere, if in a milder form, by his disciples, and the impatent rejection of all traditional restrictions on economic enterprise which was the temper of the English business world after the Civil War. In reality, the same ingredients were present throughout, but they were mixed in changing proportions, and exposed to different temperatures at different times. Like traits of individual character which are suppressed till the approach of maturity releases them, the tendencies in Puritanism, which were to make it later a potent ally of the movement against the control of economic relations in the name either of social morality or of the public interest, did not reveal themselves till political and economic changes had prepared a congenial environment for

their growth. Nor, once those condition were created, was it only England whick witnessed the transformation. In all coun tries alike, in Holland, in America, ir Scotland, in Geneva itself, the social theory of Calvinism went through the same proc ess of development. It had begun by being the very soul of authoritarian regimenta tion. It ended by being the vehicle of ar almost Utilitarian individualism. While social reformers in the sixteenth century could praise Calvin for his economic rigor their successors in Restoration England, i of one persuasion, denounced him as the parent of economic license, if of another applauded Calvinist communities for thei commercial enterprise and for their free dom from antiquated prejudices on the sub ject of economic morality. So little do those who shoot the arrows of the spirit know where they will light.

The complaint that religious radicalism which aimed at upsetting the governmen of the Church, went hand in hand with ar economic radicalism, which resented the restraints on individual self-interest im posed in the name of religion or of soca policy, was being made by the stricte school of religious opinion quite early ir

he reign of Elizabeth. Seventeenth-century
riters repeated the charge that the Puritan
onscience lost its delicacy where matters
f business were concerned, and some of
hem were sufficiently struck by the
henomenon to attempt an historical ex-
lanation of it. The example on which they
sually seized — the symbol of a supposed
eneral disposition to laxity — was the in-
ulgence shown by Puritan divines in the
articular matter of moderate interest. It
vas the effect, so the picturesque story ran,
f the Marian persecution. The refugees
vho fled to the Continent could not start
usiness in a foreign country. If, driven by
ecessity, they invested their capital and
ved on the proceeds, who could quarrel
vith so venial a lapse in so good a cause?
ubsequent writers embellished the pic-
ure. The redistribution of property at the
me of the Dissolution, and the expansion
f trade in the middle of the century, had
ed, one of them argued, to a great increase
n the volume of credit transactions. The
pprobrium which attached to loans at in-
erest — "a sly and forbid practice" —not
nly among Romanists and Anglicans, but
mong honest Puritans, played into the
ands of the less scrupulous members of
the faction." Disappointed in politics, they
ook to money-lending, and, without ven-
uring to justify usury in theory, defended
: in practice. "Without the scandal of a
ecantation, they contrived an expedient,
y maintaining that, though usury for the
ame were stark naught, yet for widows,
rphans and other impotents (therein prin-
ipally comprising the saints under perse-
ution) it was very tolerable, because profit-
ble, and in a manner necessary." Natu-
ally, Calvin's doctrine as to the legitimacy
f moderate interest was hailed by these
ypocrites with a shout of glee. "It took
vith the brethren like polygamy with the
urks, recommended by the example of
ivers zealous ministers, who themselves
esired to pass for orphans of the first rank."
Nor was it only as the apologist of moderate
nterest that Puritanism was alleged to re-
eal the cloven hoof. Puritans themselves
complained of a mercilessness in driving
hard bargains, and of a harshness to the
poor, which contrasted unfavorably with
the practice of followers of the unreformed
religion. "The Papists," wrote a Puritan
in 1653, "may rise up against many of this
generation. It is a sad thing that they should
be more forward upon a bad principle than
a Christian upon a good one."

Such, in all ages, is history as seen by the
political pamphleteer. The real story was
less dramatic, but more significant. From
the very beginning, Calvinism had comprised two elements, which Calvin himself
had fused, but which contained the seeds
of future discord. It had at once given a
whole-hearted imprimatur to the life of
business enterprise, which most earlier mor-
alists had regarded with suspicion, and had
laid upon it the restraining hand of an
inquisitorial discipline. At Geneva, where
Calvinism was the creed of a small and
homogeneous city, the second aspect had
predominated; in the many-sided life of
England, where there were numerous conflicting interests to balance it, and where it
was long politically weak, the first. Then,
in the late sixteenth and early seventeenth
centuries, had come the wave of commercial and financial expansion — companies,
colonies, capitalism in textiles, capitalism in
mining, capitalism in finance — on the
crest of which the English commercial
classes, in Calvin's day still held in leading-
strings by conservative statesmen, had
climbed to a position of dignity and af-
fluence.

Naturally, as the Puritan movement
came to its own, these two elements flew
apart. The collectivist, half-communistic aspect, which had never been acclimatized in
England, quietly dropped out of notice, to
crop up once more, and for the last time, to
the disgust and terror of merchant and
landowner, in the popular agitation under
the Commonwealth. The individualism
congenial to the world of business became
the distinctive characteristic of a Puritanism
which had arrived, and which, in becoming
a political force, was at once secularized

and committed to a career of compromise. Its note was not the attempt to establish on earth a "Kingdom of Christ," but an ideal of personal character and conduct, to be realized by the punctual discharge both of public and private duties. Its theory had been discipline; its practical result was liberty.

Given the social and political conditions of England, the transformation was inevitable. The incompatibility of Presbyterianism with the stratified arrangement of English society had been remarked by Hooker. If the City Fathers of Geneva had thrown off by the beginning of the seventeenth century the religious collectivism of Calvin's regime, it was not to be expected that the landowners and bourgeoisie of an aristocratic and increasingly commercial nation, however much Calvinist theology might appeal to them, would view with favor the social doctrines implied in Calvinist discipline. In the reign of the first two Stuarts, both economic interests and political theory pulled them hard in the opposite direction. "Merchants' doings," the man of business in Wilson's *Discourse upon Usury* had observed, "must not thus be overthwarted by preachers and others that cannot skill of their dealings." Behind the elaborate facade of Tudor State control, which has attracted the attention of historians, an individualist movement had been steadily developing, which found expression in opposition to the traditional policy of stereotyping economic relations by checking enclosure, controlling food supplies and prices, interfering with the money-market, and regulating the conditions of the wage contract and of apprenticeship. In the first forty years of the seventeenth century, on grounds both of expediency and of principle, the commercial and propertied classes were becoming increasingly restive under the whole system, at once ambitious and inefficient, of economic paternalism. It was in the same sections of the community that both religious and economic dissatisfaction were most acute. Puritanism, with its idealization of the spiritual energies which found ex-

pression in the activities of business and industry, drew the isolated rivulets of discontent together, and swept them forward with the dignity and momentum of a religious and a social philosophy.

In England, the growing disposition to apply exclusively economic standards to social relations evoked from Puritan writers and divines vigorous protests against usurious interest, extortionate prices and the oppression of tenants by landlords. The faithful, it was urged, had interpreted only too literally the doctrine that the sinner was saved, not by works, but by faith. Usury "in time of Popery an odious thing," had become a scandal. Professors, by their covetousness, caused the enemies of the reformed religion to blaspheme. The exactions of the forestaller and regrater were never so monstrous or so immune from interference. The hearts of the rich were never so hard, nor the necessities of the poor so neglected.

The poor able to work are suffered to beg; the impotent, aged and sick are not sufficiently provided for, but almost starved with the allowance of 3d. and 4d. apiece a week. . . These are the last times indeed. Men generally are all for themselves. And some would set up such, having a form of religion, without the power of it.

These utterances came, however, from that part of the Puritan mind which looked backward. That which looked forward found in the rapidly growing spirit of economic enterprise something not uncongenial to its own temper, and went out to welcome it as an ally. What in Calvin had been a qualified concession to practical exigencies appeared in some of his later followers as a frank idealization of the life of the trader, as the service of God and the training-ground of the soul. Discarding the suspicion of economic motives, which had been as characteristic of the reformer as of medieval theologians, Puritanism in its later phases added a halo of ethical sanctification to the appeal of economic expediency, and offered a moral creed, in which the duties of religion and the call business ended their long estrangement an unanticipated reconciliation. Its okesmen pointed out, it is true, the peril the soul involved in a single-minded ncentration on economic interests. The emy, however, was not riches, but the d habits sometimes associated with them, d its warnings against an excessive pre-cupation with the pursuit of gain wore ore and more the air of afterthoughts, ap-nded to teaching, the main tendency and phasis of which were little affected by ese incidental qualifications. It insisted, short, that money-making, if not free om spiritual dangers, was not a danger d nothing else, but that it could be, and ght to be, carried on for the greater glory God.

The conception to which it appealed to idge the gulf sprang from the very heart Puritan theology. It was that expressed the characteristic and oft-used phrase, "a lling." The rational order of the universe the work of God, and its plan requires at the individual should labor for God's ory. There is a spiritual calling, and a mporal calling. It is the first duty of the ristian to know and believe in God; it by faith that he will be saved. But faith not a mere profession, such as that of lkative of Prating Row, whose "religion to make a noise." The only genuine faith the faith which produces works.

the day of Doom men shall be judged ac-rding to their fruits. It will not be said en, Did you believe? but, Were you doers, talkers only?

he second duty of the Christian is to labor the affairs of practical life, and this sec-d duty is subordinate only to the first. iod," wrote a Puritan divine,

th call every man and woman . . . to ve him in some peculiar employment in is world, both for their own and the com-on good. . . . The Great Governour of the rld hath appointed to every man his proper st and province, and let him be never so tive out of his sphere, he will be at a great

loss, if he do not keep his own vineyard and mind his own business.

From this reiterated insistence on secular obligations as imposed by the divine will, it follows that, not withdrawal from the world, but the conscientious discharge of the duties of business, is among the loftiest of religious and moral virtues.

The begging friars and such monks as live only to themselves and to their formal devotion, but do employ themselves in no one thing to further their own subsistence or the good of mankind . . . yet have the confidence to boast of this their course as a state of perfection; which in very deed, as to the worthiness of it, falls short of the poorest cobbler, for his is a calling of God, and theirs is none.

The idea was not a new one. Luther had advanced it as a weapon against monasticism. But for Luther, with his patriarchal outlook on economic affairs, the calling means normally that state of life in which the individual has been set by Heaven, and against which it is impiety to rebel. On the lips of Puritan divines, it is not an invitation to resignation, but the bugle-call which summons the elect to the long battle which will end only with their death. "The world is all before them." They are to hammer out their salvation, not merely *in vocatione*, but *per vocationem*. The calling is not a condition in which the individual is born, but a strenuous and exacting enterprise, to be undertaken, indeed, under the guidance of Providence, but to be chosen by each man for himself, with a deep sense of his solemn responsibilities.

God hath given to man reason for this use, that he should first consider, then choose, then put in execution; and it is a preposterous and brutish thing to fix or fall upon any weighty business, such as a calling or condition of life, without a careful pondering it in the balance of sound reason.

Laborare est orare.[1] By the Puritan mor-

[1] To work is to pray. [Ed. note]

alist the ancient maxim is repeated with a new and intenser significance. The labor which he idealizes is not simply a requirement imposed by nature, or a punishment for the sin of Adam. It is itself a kind of ascetic discipline, more rigorous than that demanded of any order of mendicants — a discipline imposed by the will of God, and to be undergone, not in solitude, but in the punctual discharge of secular duties. It is not merely an economic means, to be laid aside when physical needs have been satisfied. It is a spiritual end, for in it alone can the soul find health, and it must be continued as an ethical duty long after it has ceased to be a material necessity. Work thus conceived stands at the very opposite pole from "good works," as they were understood, or misunderstood, by Protestants. They, it was thought, had been a series of single transactions, performed as compensation for particular sins, or out of anxiety to acquire merit. What is required of the Puritan is not individual meritorious acts, but a holy life — a system in which every element is grouped round a central idea, the service of God, from which all disturbing irrelevances have been pruned, and to which all minor interests are subordinated.

Social development moves with a logic whose inferences are long delayed, and the day of these remoter applications had not yet dawned. The version of Christian ethics expounded by Puritanism in some of its later phases was still only in its vigorous youth. But it sailed forward on a flowing tide. It had an unconscious ally in the preoccupation with economic interests which found expression in the enthusiasm of business politicians for a commercial *Machtpolitik*.[2] The youthful Commonwealth, a rival of Holland "for the fairest mistress in the world — trade," was not two years old when it made its own essay in economic imperialism. "A bare-faced war" for commerce, got up by the Royal African Company, was Clarendon's verdict on the Dutch war of 1665–7. Five years later, Shaftes-

bury hounded the City against Holla? with the cry of *Delenda est Carthago*.[3] T? war finance of the Protectorate had made necessary for Cromwell to court Dutch a? Jewish, as well as native, capitalists, a? the impecunious Government of the Res? ration was in the hands of those syndicat of goldsmiths whose rapacity the Chanc? lor, a survivor from the age before t? deluge, when aristocrats still despised t? upstart plutocracy, found not a little d gusting.

The contemporary progress of econom thought fortified no less the mood whi? glorified the economic virtues. Econom science developed in England, not, as Germany, as the handmaid of public a ministration, nor, as in France, through t? speculations of philosophers and men letters, but as the interpreter of the practic interests of the City. With the excepti? of Petty and Locke, its most eminent prac tioners were business men, and the que tions which excited them were those, n? ther of production nor of social organizatic but of commerce and finance — the balan of trade, tariffs, interest, currency a? credit. The rise of Political Arithmetic ? ter the Restoration, profoundly influence as it was, by the Cartesian philosophy a? by the progress of natural science, stamp? their spontaneous and doctrineless indivi ualism with the seal of theoretical orth doxy. "Knowledge," wrote the author the preface to a work by one of the mc eminent exponents of the new science, "? great measure is become mechanical." T? exact analysis of natural conditions, t? calculations of forces and stains, the ? duction of the complex to the operation simple, constant and measurable forces, w the natural bias of an age interested p? marily in mathematics and physics. ? object was

to express itself in terms of number, weight measure, to use only arguments of sense, a? to consider only such causes as have visib

---

[2] Power politics. [Ed. note]

[3] Carthage must be destroyed. [Ed. note]

foundations in nature; leaving those that depend upon the mutable minds, opinions, appetites and passions of particular men to the consideration of others.

In such an atmosphere, the moral casuistry, which had occupied so large a place in the earlier treatment of social and economic subjects, seemed the voice of an antiquated superstition. Moreover, the main economic dogma of the mercantilist had an affinity with the main ethical dogma of the Puritan, which was the more striking because the coincidence was undesigned. To the former, production, not consumption, was the pivot of the economic system, and, by what seems to the modern reader a curious perversion, consumption is applauded only because it offers a new market for productive energies. To the latter, the cardinal virtues are precisely those which find in the strenuous toils of industry and commerce their most natural expression. The typical qualities of the successful business life, in the days before the rise of joint-stock enterprise, were intensity and earnestness of labor, concentration, system and method, the initiative which broke with routine and the foresight which postponed the present to the future.

To such a generation, a creed which transformed the acquisition of wealth from a drudgery or a temptation into a moral duty was the milk of lions. It was not that religion was expelled from practical life, but that religion itself gave it a foundation of granite. In that keen atmosphere of economic enterprise, the ethics of the Puritan bore some resemblance to those associated later with the name of Smiles. The good Christian was not wholly dissimilar from the economic man. . . .

Puritanism and the Spirit of Capitalism

WINTHROP S. HUDSON

In the following essay, Professor Winthrop S. Hudson (1911–   ), of the Colgate-Rochester Divinity School, concerns himself with Tawney's work and Puritanism in general. A penetrating student of English and American church history Professor Hudson has been a prolific writer on various facets of religious history. He is past president of the American Society of Church History and holds the Ph.D. degree in history as well as the Bachelor of Divinity degree.

CALVINISM as an historical movement was exceedingly complex. It was a phenomenon in which theology, economic theory, political philosophy, and a general cultural orientation were inextricably mixed and applied in an intense effort to refashion society into a Holy Commonwealth. In attempting to interpret this movement, as Sidney E. Mead has pointed out, "one is always in danger either of trying to do complete justice to the complexity and landing in a confusing incoherence and lack of clarity, or of seizing upon one interpretative theme in the interest of clarity and landing in over-simplification." Most of the discussions of Calvinism, in any or all of its various manifestations, have avoided the first alternative — falling into the morass of con-

From Winthrop S. Hudson, "Puritanism and the Spirit of Capitalism," *Church History*, Vol. XVIII (March, 1949), pp. 3–17. By permission of the author and the editors of *Church History*.

fusion and incoherence — but many have succumbed to the second — an over-simplification that is definitely misleading.

It is now generally acknowledged that Max Weber's attempt to explain the economic significance of Calvinism is a particularly conspicuous illustration of such over-simplification. It is not so generally recognized that R. H. Tawney, in his *Religion and the Rise of Capitalism,* has not entirely escaped the slanting of his material. This may be due partly to the fact that it was Tawney who exposed Weber's most glaring over-simplifications. A more fundamental reason for the failure to question some of Tawney's conclusions is that the distortion involved in his thesis is very subtle, and the thesis itself is carefully qualified, and on the whole quite sound. Nevertheless, the overall impression as to the nature and character of the Puritan movement is somewhat misleading.

The problem to which both Weber and Tawney addressed themselves was the remarkable coincidence of a particular religious affiliation with a particular social status; specifically, the identification of Calvinism with the industrial and commercial classes of the new centers of capitalist activity. "By the middle of the seventeenth century," writes Tawney in his Foreword to the English translation of Weber's work, "the contrast between the social conservatism of Catholic Europe and the strenuous enterprise of Calvinist communities had become a commonplace." As a result of his examination of the evidence, Weber set forth the thesis that Calvinism was the parent of modern capitalism. Tawney, reexamining Weber's thesis some twenty years later, concluded that, while Calvinism was not exactly the parent of capitalism, it was, in its seventeenth-century English version, at least the handmaiden of capitalism.

Weber contended that Calvinism created the psychological climate which was the indispensable prerequisite to the rise of modern capitalism. Without a seemingly irrational spirit of unlimited lust for gain as an end in itself and not related to the satisfaction of human needs, modern capitalism could never have developed.

A man does not "by nature" wish to earn more and more money, but simply to live as he is accustomed to live and to earn as much as is necessary for that purpose.

It was, asserted Weber, such an irrational and unnatural spirit that Calvinism fostered; and by emphasizing the economic virtues of industry, diligence, frugality, sobriety, and prudence as spiritual ends, Calvinism welded the feeble thrust of the aspiring bourgeoisie into a disciplined force that was able to transform an entire culture and to set its stamp on every aspect of society. The dynamic that supplied the motive power for the strenuous activity and seemingly limitless energy which characterized the typical Protestant ascetic, Weber maintained, was to be found in the peculiarly Calvinist concept of "the calling."

Labor . . . became not simply an economic means but a spiritual end, and ultimately it became an end in itself. The key to this shift, Weber maintains, is the fact that success in one's calling was interpreted as a sign of God's blessing, and thus evidence of one's election. In commercial life success came to be measured more and more in terms of financial profit, and "the pursuit of riches, which once had been feared as the enemy of religion, was now welcomed as its ally." In the end, this led to "the temper of single-minded concentration on pecuniary gain," which is what Weber understands by his phrase — the spirit of capitalism.

Tawney criticized Weber at several points, principally in terms of his over-simplifications.

It is the temptation of one who expounds a new and fruitful idea to use it as a key to unlock all doors, and to explain by reference to a single principle phenomena which are, in reality, the result of several converging causes.

Tawney pointed out that Weber ignored or touched too lightly on other "intellectual movements, which were favorable to the growth of business enterprise and to an individualist attitude towards economic relations, but which had little to do with religion," and that he sought "to explain by reference to moral and intellectual influences developments which have their principal explanation in another region altogether." Tawney's major contribution to the discussion, however, was to emphasize that causation can work in two directions. "Is it not a little artificial," he asks, "to suggest that capitalist enterprise had to wait, as Weber appears to imply, till religious changes had produced a capitalist spirit?" It would be equally plausible "to argue that the religious changes were themselves merely the result of economic movements." Instead of Calvinism producing the capitalist spirit, both can with "equal plausibility be regarded as different effects of changes in economic organization and social structure." Actually what occurred, Tawney maintained, was that, while Calvinism helped mould the social order, it was in turn moulded by it.

Weber's failure to give due weight to the reciprocal nature of causation led him into a further over-simplification — the equation of seventeenth-century Puritanism with sixteenth-century Calvinism. Tawney pointed out that "most of Weber's illustrations of his thesis are drawn from the writings of the English Puritans of the latter part of the seventeenth century," a fact which Weber readily admits. Weber proceeded on the assumption that, for his purposes, "ascetic Protestantism" can be treated "as a single whole," which finds its clearest expression among the English Puritans of the late seventeenth century. This assumption, Tawney insisted, cannot be defended. Under the impact of new economic conditions, a profound change had taken place. The Calvinists of the sixteenth century believed in a rigorous discipline, and the economic individualism which both Tawney and Weber ascribe to the Puritan movement in its later phases would have "horrified" them.

Like Weber, Tawney finds the key to the separation of economic from ethical interests in what they both considered "the very heart of Puritan theology" — the Calvinist conception of "the calling." Applied to commercial life, it meant that "poverty . . . was not a misfortune to be pitied and relieved, but a moral failing to be condemned," and that riches were "the blessing which rewards the triumph of energy and will."

By a kind of happy, preëstablished harmony . . . , success in business is in itself almost a sign of spiritual grace, for it is a proof that a man has labored faithfully in his vocation, and that "God has blessed his trade."

Ethical distinctions in commercial life were thus obliterated, and the service of Mammon came to be identified with service to God.

Weber confessed that such a gross interpretation of "the calling" could not be found in the writings of John Calvin. Indeed, it was definitely rejected by him. But Weber felt that, if Calvin had not, then his followers, on the basis of psychological necessity, must have made such an interpretation, and Tawney, as we have seen, was convinced that such a conception revealed itself in the second half of the seventeenth century as the dominating feature of Puritan thought. Unfortunately, both men failed to realize that such an interpretation not only isolated the doctrine of the calling from its larger context in Calvinist thought, but it completely subverted the fundamental theological structure of Calvinism. Nor did they recognize that such an interpretation was not necessary as an explanation of the strenuous and energetic activity displayed by the Puritans in commercial life.

The failure to go to the root of Calvinism, even in its seventeenth-century English version, meant that its most characteristic feature was ignored and neglected —

namely, a preoccupation with God as the supreme good, and the only worthy end, indeed, the necessary end — of all endeavor. "What is the chief end of man?" asks the Westminster Shorter Cathechism. "Man's chief end is to glorify God and enjoy him forever." Incredible as it may seem to the modern mind, the Puritan held that God is more important than business, art, poetry, pleasure, or any of the other possible "goods" of life. It was almost an obsession, and the depth of this religious interest is reflected in even the most casual correspondence. God was, indeed, the be-all and end-all of existence, and the establishment of a right relationship to him was "the pearl of great price" without which all else was but dross.

If one is to serve God with singleness of heart and mind, quite obviously the reconciliation of God and Mammon is exceedingly difficult. In the Christian tradition, the first and great commandment has as its authoritative corollary, "a second like unto it: Thou shalt love thy neighbor as thyself." What is theoretically impossible has not always been practically impossible, and it must be confessed that the second commandment has been, on occasion, the subject of artful rationalization by the servants of Mammon. The question, of course, is one of priority, and there can be little doubt as to where the convinced Puritan stood, even in the latter part of the seventeenth century.

Post-Restoration Puritanism is the source from whence Weber drew most of his illustrations, and it is the particular phase of Calvinism on which Tawney rested his case. Of the post-Restoration Puritans both Weber and Tawney gave primary attention to Richard Baxter. Weber placed Baxter "at the center of the discussion," since he "stands out above many other writers on Puritan ethics, both because of his eminently practical and realistic attitude, and, at the same time, because of the universal recognition accorded to his works, which have gone through many new editions and translations." Tawney, following Weber's lead, gave equally prominent attention to Baxter as "the most learned, the most practical, and the most persuasive" of the champions of Puritanism in the last half of the seventeenth century. It would not seem unfair, therefore, to examine the Weber Tawney thesis in the light of Richard Baxter's thought.

If any one thing is clear in the writing of Richard Baxter, it is his intensely anti Mammon spirit. He constantly insists that God and Mammon are antithetical, and he lashes out against the hypocrisy of those who think that they can be reconciled.

Take heed that you think not of reconciling God and mammon, and mixing heaven and earth to be your felicity, and of dreaming that you may keep heaven for a reserve at last, when the world hath been loved as your best so long as you could keep it.

If thy belly be thy god and the world be thy heaven, then serve and seek them (and pretend not to be a Christian).

When seeming Christians are as worldly and ambitious as others and make as great a matter of their gain and wealth and honor, it showeth that they do but cover the base and sordid spirit of worldliness with the visor of the Christian name to deceive themselves, and bring the faith of Christians into scorn, and dishonor the holy name which they usurp.

The person who seeks riches is

like a foolish traveler who, having a day's journey to go, doth spend all the day in gathering together a load of meat and clothes and money, more than he can carry, for fear of wanting by the way; or like a foolish runner that hath a race to run for his life and spends the time in which he should be running gathering a burden of pretended necessaries. You have all the while God's work to do and your souls to mind and judgment to prepare for, and you are tiring and vexing yourselves for unnecessary things, as if it were the top of your ambition to be able to say, in hell, that you died rich.

Prosperity, Baxter insists, is no sign of God's favor, nor is poverty evidence of his displeasure.

Take heed that you judge not of God's love, or of your happiness or misery, by your riches or poverty, prosperity or adversity, as knowing that they come alike to all, and love or hatred is not to be discerned by them. . . . A carnal mind will judge of its own happiness and the love of God by carnal things because it savoreth not spiritual mercies, but grace giveth a Christian another judgment.

Indeed, far from being an indication of spiritual grace, one's own prosperity is frequently a temptation of the devil, for men thereby "think God, when he prospereth them, is not so angry with them as preachers tell them." It is the devil, not God, who "is exceeding diligent to get the wealth and prosperity of the world on his side that he may not seem to flatter his servants with promises but to reward them with real felicity and wealth."

In any vocation, the person who makes private gain his goal denies the end of his calling. One must constantly "take heed lest, under pretense of diligence in your calling, you be drawn to earthly-mindedness, and excessive cares or covetous designs for rising in the world." Many a man deceives himself by thinking that "he is no worldling because he useth no unlawful means but the labor of his calling to grow rich." The lawyer is warned to

be sure that you make not the getting of money to be the principal end in the exercise of your function but the promoting of justice . . . and therein the pleasing of the most righteous God. For your work can be no better than your end. A base end doth debase your work. . . . Make the cause of the innocent as it were your own and suffer it not to miscarry through your slothfulness and neglect. He is a lover of money more than justice that will sweat in the cause of the rich that pay him well and will slubber over and starve the cause of the poor because he getteth little by them.

Physicians are admonished to

be sure that the saving of men's lives and health be first and chiefly your intention before any gain or honor of your own . . . Be ready to help the poor as well as the rich. . . . Let not the health or lives of men be neglected because they have no money to give you.

Nor is the businessman exempt. In making a bargain or contract, the businessman must set his heart upon the true love of his neighbor and ask himself: "How would I be dealt with myself, if my case were the same with his?" Instead of thinking of his own gain, he must remember how much more he will lose by sin. He must consider his neighbor's situation, whether or not he can afford it, and he must not believe every common report of his neighbor's riches. He must regard the public good above his own commodity, for "it is not lawful to take up or keep up any oppressing monopoly or trade which tendeth to enrich you by the loss of the commonwealth or the many." He must give "special respect to the common estimate and to the market price." He must not quibble over prices, nor bargain more than necessary. In doubtful cases, he is told to "choose that side which is safest to the peace of your consciences hereafter, though it be against your commodity."

The one statement from the writings of Baxter which Weber and Tawney are able to use effectively in support of their thesis that Puritanism sanctified the pursuit of riches and thus led to the obliteration of ethical values in economic life is the much quoted sentence:

If God show you a way in which you may lawfully get more than in another way (without wrong to your soul, or to any other), if you refuse this, and choose the less gainful way, you cross one of the ends of your calling, and you refuse to be God's steward, and to accept his gifts, and use them for him when he requireth it. You may labor to be rich for God, though not for the flesh and sin.

This is a perfect illustration of the distortion involved in isolating the concept of "the calling" from its context. Tawney, ignoring even the qualification within the quotation itself, makes the blunt assertion that "so far from poverty being meritorious, it is a duty to choose the more profitable occupation." It is true, as Baxter says elsewhere, that "the largest stock must be accepted and used for God when he trusteth us with it," but this is a subordinate principle and cannot be generalized into a bald injunction to "get all you can."

The particular quotation from Baxter, cited by Weber and Tawney, concerning the choice of a vocation is actually only one of a series of directions devoted to this problem. In choosing a trade or calling, writes Baxter, the first consideration is "the service of God and the public good, and therefore that calling which most conduceth to the public good is to be preferred." Second, "when two callings equally conduce to the public good, and one of them hath the advantage of riches and the other is more advantageous to your souls, the latter must be preferred." For "next to the public good, the soul's advantage must guide your choice." One must also think of his physical and mental health, and if possible

choose a calling which so exerciseth the body as not to overwhelm you with cares and labor and deprive you of all leisure for the holy and noble employments of the mind, and which so exerciseth your mind as to allow you some exercise for the body also.

It is only after carefully considering what one is "fittest for, both in mind and body" and finding that two possible vocations are equally conducive to the public good, the soul's advantage, and the health of mind and body, that it is

lawful and meet to look at the commodity of your calling. Though it is said, Prov. xxiii. 4, "Labor not to be rich," the meaning is that you make not riches your chief end: riches for our fleshly ends must not ultimately be intended or sought. But in subordination to higher things they may; that is, you may labor in that manner as tendeth most to your success and lawful gain: you are bound to im-

prove all your Master's talents. But then your end must be that you may be the better provided to do God's service and may do the more good with what you have. If God show you a way in which you may lawfully get more than in another way (without wrong to your soul or any other), if you refuse this, and choose the less gainful way, you cross one of the ends of your calling, and you refuse to be God's steward, and to accept his gifts, and use them for him when he requireth it. You may labor to be rich for God, though not for the flesh and sin.

In the light of the prior considerations to be faced and the restrictions which surrounded commercial pursuits, and in the light of the fact that each individual was to be held personally accountable to God for the decisions he had reached, this direction "to improve all your Master's talents" does not represent a very significant concession to Mammon. Actually, as Baxter makes clear elsewhere, even under these circumstances, riches were not so much to be sought as to be regretfully accepted. The more profitable calling could not be pursued in any lighthearted manner or with a comfortable assurance that it constituted an easy and safe path to the narrow gate that openeth unto life. Always remember, Baxter counsels, that riches

are in themselves but dross, which will leave thee at the grave as poor as any. And as to their usefulness, they are but thy Master's talents, and the more thou hast the greater will be thine account. And very few rich men escape the snare and come to heaven.

Since riches are "the commonest cause of men's damnation" and "make it much harder for a man to be saved," they ought to be avoided if possible. When you realize, says Baxter, that you must make "a daily reckoning how you lay out all that God committeth to your trust," it will "quench your thirst after plenty and prosperity." You will become more concerned "to use well what you have than to get more."

"The first characteristic to strike the modern reader in all this teaching," conesses Tawney in discussing Baxter, "is its conservatism." But then he goes on to suggest that

these utterances came . . . from that part of the Puritan mind which looked backward. That which looked forward found in the rapidly growing spirit of economic enterprise something not uncongenial to its own temper, and went out to welcome it as an ally. What in Calvin had been a qualified concession to practical exigencies appeared in some of his later followers as a frank idealization of the life of the trader, as the service of God and the training ground of the soul.

Tawney, therefore, dismisses Baxter and his like-minded contemporaries as anachronisms, and finds the true Puritan spirit revealed in a man like Richard Steele, who was adjusting himself to the ideas and ideals of the new Political Arithmetic. What Tawney fails to see is that when these new elements gained the upper hand, Puritanism ceased to be Puritanism. They represent the infiltration of a spirit which the convinced Puritan did not hesitate to label pagan and anti-Christian. Far from being the logical flowering of certain inherent tendencies in Puritanism, the economic ethics which increasingly dominated English commercial and business life toward the close of the seventeenth century were the very antithesis of those which were fundamental to the whole Puritan outlook. Their acceptance by nominal Puritans is an illustration of the attrition to which any idealistic movement is subject, and it marked the crumbling of the foundation upon which the Puritan structure rested. The victory of the spirit of capitalism in a very real sense meant the defeat of Puritanism.

Nor was the Puritan ethic mere pious verbiage. "The fundamental question," Tawney observes," . . . is not what kind of rules a faith enjoins, but what type of character it esteems and cultivates." His contention, however, that "the rules of Christian morality elaborated by Baxter" found no response in souls awakened by Puritan preaching is patently absurd to anyone at all acquainted with Puritanism. It is not true that the Puritan character offered "but a polished surface on which these ghostly admonitions could find no enduring foothold." The few illustrations which Tawney gives of a sensitive and aggressive Puritan conscience were not exceptional and can be multiplied many times. To be sure, when the religious foundations crumbled and the spiritual vitality of the movement disappeared, the ethical injunctions, which derived their force from a vivid faith in God as a righteous judge, quite naturally lost their compelling power.

It should be apparent, as a result of this discussion, that the dynamic, which gave impetus to the tremendous Puritan drive in vocational activity, was not rooted in the Puritan conception of "the calling," but rather in the larger context of the Calvinist conception of God and of man's relationship to Him. God is the Lord — the "Owner," Baxter calls him — and man is his steward. As God's steward, man is accountable to God for two things — his time and his possessions. For the best possible use of every moment and every penny, he is personally responsible to God. Both time and money, therefore, must be redeemed in terms of being devoted to the highest possible good at any particular moment. Parasites, who live in idleness or in "unprofitable callings," are unfaithful stewards. In like manner, one stands in perpetual judgment with reference to the use he makes of his money. As a faithful steward he must shun needless luxury and ostentatious display, not because they are sinful in themselves, but because the money they require can be put to a better use, either in charitable activities or productive enterprises.

Emphasizing as they did the economic virtues of diligence and thrift as religious duties, it was inevitable that the Puritans should prosper and advance in economic status. It was also natural, since they were excluded by legislation from participating in public affairs and educational pursuits, that they should be found in disproportionate numbers among those engaged in commercial life. Nor is it surprising that Puritanism won its recruits mainly from among the merchants, lawyers, and small landholders.

The middle class was less bound by tradition than the other classes of society and thus was more receptive to new religious ideas, and the virile character of Puritanism was the type of religious discipline that would appeal to any spiritually sensitive spirits who were engaged in the strenuous struggle of a rising class to make a place for itself in society. But this does not mean that Puritanism was primarily a middle class movement which rationalized and perpetuated middle class ideals.

The disintegration of the Puritan movement after the Restoration was relatively rapid. The religious zeal of its adherents was subject to the debilitating effect of the passing of time. Their moral idealism was subject to the inevitable attrition of the world, and they were exposed to pressures and temptations generated by the very prosperity which Puritanism tended to foster among its adherents. In the end, there were shepherds who did not hesitate to do violence to the inner integrity of the entire Puritan intellectual system in order to maintain their flocks by a frank appeal to self-interest. But the adjustment to the world and to the ethics of a bourgeois society was not an easy or a happy adjustment. . . .

Exploiting Bourgeois

CHRISTOPHER HILL

Except for a time during the Second World War while in the military and foreign office, Christopher Hill (1912–   ) has been a fellow and tutor in Modern History at Balliol College, Oxford. A prolific writer, Professor Hill's main work has been concerned with the economic problems of the Church of England in the last half century before the Civil War. *The English Revolution*, published in 1940, was intended as a Marxist textbook, and his latest work, *The Intellectual Origins of the English Revolution*, attacks Puritanism as a myth.

I N SEPTEMBER 1641 the House of Commons voted,

It shall be lawful for the parishioners of any parish . . . to set up a lecture, and to maintain an orthodox minister at their own charge to preach every Lord's Day where there is no preaching, and to preach one day in every week where there is no weekly lecture.

This was a double-edged weapon, intended partly to allow parishioners to force lec-

turers of their own choosing on Laudian or "dumb dog" incumbents; partly to steal the thunder of the unauthorised "mechanick preachers" who were collecting congregations outside the parish churches. Numbers of parishes took advantage of the order, often after keen struggles, in which the House of Commons intervened to insist the ministers must allow free use of their pulpits to lecturers. "Furious promoters of the most dangerous innovations," Charles I

From Christopher Hill, *The Century of Revolution*, 1603–1714 (London, 1961), pp. 162–173. Reprinted by permission of Thomas Nelson and Sons Limited.

alled lecturers; their prayers and sermons 'stir up and continue the rebellion raised gainst me." Lecturers and ministers frequently acted as recruiting agents and propagandists. In August 1643 the House of Commons ordered "divers godly ministers" o go "into divers counties . . . to possess he people with the truth and justice of he Parliament's cause in taking up of defensive arms." Meanwhile the Commons ejected numbers of "scandalous ministers," many for reasons which made them scandalous in the modern sense, but others because of their political attitude. Ejected clergy were allowed one-fifth of the parochial revenue, at the expense of their successors. As the Parliamentary armies advanced, so the purge advanced with them; until finally, under the Committees for the Propagation of the Gospel in Wales and the North Parts, groups of itinerant ministers were set up to carry the Puritan gospel into the hitherto "dark corners" of the land. So the state took over the task which the Feoffees for Impropriations had begun twenty-five years earlier. Church building, neglected for a century and a half, was resumed in the fifties — especially in the north and west — at government expense.

The other aspect of the Feoffees' work, augmentation of livings, was also resumed on a vastly expanded scale. Bishops' lands were sold under an ordinance of 1646, Dean and Chapter lands in 1649. The original Puritan hope of devoting the whole of the proceeds to the promotion of religion and learning was not realised: the demands of the Army were too great. Nevertheless, over £30,000 a year from Dean and Chapter lands went to augment stipends of ministers and schoolmasters. More important, Royalists were allowed to redeem part of their fine by settling impropriated tithes (if they owned any) on the vicar of the parish. From these two sources, and much greater sums from municipal and private generosity, a large number of the English clergy must have enjoyed far more substantial incomes than before 1640 or after 1660.

Before 1640 there had been considerable resentment at the Laudian attempt to increase tithe payments. Now the whole principle of tithes was challenged. The minister should depend on the voluntary contributions of his parishioners, it was claimed: otherwise he was a "hireling." If voluntary contributions were not sufficient, why should the minister not work like anyone else? The Reformation doctrine of the priesthood of all believers would be carried to its logical conclusion by the abolition of a privileged caste of clergy.

These arguments carried vast political and economic consequences. If tithes were not paid to ministers, then they would not be paid to lay impropriators either. Would these lay owners receive compensation, and if so at whose expense? Or would they merely be expropriated? Few of the propertied class regarded either proposal with anything but alarm. An established church stood or fell with tithes. Election and payment of ministers by congregations would mean the end of any nationally controlled and disciplined church. It would make anything but complete religious toleration virtually impossible. The reasons for preserving a national church were social as well as religious. Thus in 1650 Alderman Violet, in a report to a Parliamentary committee on the decay of trade, proposed as remedies,

First, to settle able and godly ministers in all churches throughout the nation, that will teach the people to fear God, to obey their superiors, and to live peaceably with each other, with a competent subsistence for all such ministers.

The social function of religion was not often so frankly expressed, but many men undoubtedly agreed with Alderman Violet. Abolition of a state Church would be an act of expropriation. Many thousands of gentlemen enjoyed rights of patronage to livings, for which they or their ancestors had paid hard cash. They did not wish to lose the right to appoint to these livings their younger sons, brothers, tutors, chaplains, or other dependents; nor to be deprived at the same stroke of the squire's faithful ally, the parson. Sir William Strickland spoke for many impropriators when he said in Parliament in June 1657, "The same levelling principle will lay waste properties and deny rents, upon the same account that they do tithes." Tithes, a pamphlet said in 1641, were paid especially by "the meanest and poorest people"; "the richest citizen in London hardly paying so much as a countryman that hath but £20 or £10 a year in his occupation." Opponents of tithes came from the middling and poorer sort; the rich suffered comparatively little, and might even be recipients of tithes. These are some of the reasons why the question of tithes aroused the deepest passions and proved the most bitter of all the issues which divided radical from conservative Parliamentarians.

The threat to tithes must have seemed very real. They were opposed not only by Levellers, the Barebones Parliament, and the more radical sects, but also, and insistently, by a respectable civil servant like Milton, by the Lieutenant-General in Ireland, Edmund Ludlow, and by very many in the Army. Cromwell himself was alleged to have promised at Dunbar that if God gave him the victory he would abolish tithes. Tithes survived; but ministers abandoned the claim to collect them by divine right. The law of the land was a safer plea. One reason for the survival of tithes was the view, accepted by all parties, that very few ministers would be maintained by voluntary contributions if legal compulsion was removed. "The minister," wrote Blyth in 1652, "might go barefoot, and his family a-begging, for what the common people would contribute to his subsistence." We must remember remarks like this (and many could be quoted) whenever we are tempted to think that the seventeenth century was "a more religious age" than the present.

Historians these days are cautious about the labels "Presbyterian" and "Independent." In November 1641, after sitting a year in the House of Commons, Sir Edward Dering said,

I have not yet heard any one gentleman within these walls stand up and assert his thought here for either of these ways [Presbyterian or Independent].

Many "Independent" members became elders when Presbyterianism was the established Church; many who voted for a Presbyterian establishment in 1646 were moderate Episcopalians or conservative Erastians, choosing the lesser evil. Haslerig, one of the "Independent" leaders, was, in Clarendon's words, "as to religion perfectly Presbyterian." In political usage, "Presbyterian" meant conservative Parliamentarian, "Independent" one who favoured religious toleration. Or, as an anonymous Royalist pamphleteer put it,

He that would rightly understand them must read for Presbytery, aristocracy; and democracy, for Independency.

The Presbyterian establishment was virtually still-born. By the time it reached the statute book (1646) power was passing to the "Independent" Army. Only in London and Lancashire was there much support from below for the Presbyterian system. Parliament had been careful to insist on its own absolute control of the Church centrally, and had nominated the ruling elders who were to function locally. When the Assembly of Divines proclaimed that ministers and elders held their power from Jesus Christ, the House of Commons was quick to point out that, on the contrary, they held it from Parliament. *Jure divino* doctrines were as unwelcome in new presbyter as they had been in Archbishop Laud. There was little danger here of "a Pope in every parish." The "Independents" also favoured a state Church, but with very loosely defined doctrine, with tithes maintained or replaced by some certain form of maintenance for ministers, and with toleration of law-abiding sects. Religious toleration, which has come to be thought of as the hall-mark of "Independency," was forced upon the "Independent" members of Parliament by political necessity. The Independent churches in New England were very far from tolerant. But the sects included the most radical and determined opponents of King and Bishops. Cromwell found that toleration (for those with "the root of the matter" in them) created the best possible fighting morale; the members of Parliament who forced through the Self-Denying Ordinance and the New Model Army needed the political support of the sectaries.

For conservatives, religious toleration was anathema. It meant that the lower orders could collect together and discuss whatever they liked, with no control from above at all. Professor Notestein has suggested that the sectaries brought Christianity to some of the poorer classes who had previously never gone to church; but their main influence was among the urban lower middle class. Edward's *Gangraena*, published in 1646, is a hysterical but reasonably accurate denunciation of the errors of the sectaries. Many of the heresies he pilloried are as political as "Further error No. 52 — By natural birth all men are equally and alike born to like property, liberty and freedom." The idea of a single state Church was so deeply embedded in most men's thought that freedom to choose one's religion seemed in itself subversive. All respectable citizens knew that it was the duty of heads of households to bring up their servants in sound religious principles. But if apprentices and journeymen might go to a different church from their masters, who knew what nonsensical notions they might not hear, or even preach? There could be no good order under such a system. Most sects elected their own ministers and discussed church business in a democratic manner; they formed schools of self-government. The theological starting-point of, say, the Baptists, was subversive of a state Church. For adult baptism meant

that each individual, when he reached the years of discretion, decided for himself what Church he would belong to. It denied that every child born in England automatically became a member of the Church of England. So no Baptist could logically pay tithes voluntarily. In general the sects seem especially to have appealed to women, to whom some of them gave equal rights. Again this seemed to conservatives subversive of natural subordination, and productive of nothing but family strife. Women gained immeasurably in status during this period, thanks not only to the greater equality they enjoyed in sectarian congregations but also to economic activities forced on them by the absence of husbands on military service or in exile.

There was a lunatic fringe of self-appointed Messiahs, like Lodowick Muggleton, who damned his rivals with cheerful gusto, and John Robins, who believed he was God Almighty and proposed to lead 144,000 men to reconquer the Holy Land. There were Ranters, some of whom believed that God's grace had made them incapable of sin, and acted upon that belief. But there were also very many who described themselves as Seekers, who tried all Churches and were satisfied with none, men like the Leveller William Walwyn who specialised in Socratic questioning. Seekers and Ranters were not very numerous outside London and the Army, but they seemed to prove the point so laboured by conservatives, that toleration could only lead to scepticism, atheism, and debauchery. Calvinist theology taught that the mass of mankind was sinful: unless preached at and disciplined by their betters they were bound to go astray. Democracy must lead to heresy. "That the major vote of the people should ordinarily be just and good is next to an impossibility," wrote Richard Baxter in 1659. "All this stir of the Republicans is but to make the seed of the Serpent to be the sovereign rulers of the earth." The greatest heresy of all was that Christ died for all men, that all had a spark of the divine in them, and so, that all men were equal. The Quakers were more interested in religion than in politics; but any Justice of the Peace or member of Parliament could see that to say "thou" to social superiors, to refuse to remove one's hat to constituted authority was neither merely religious nor a harmless eccentricity in the explosive political atmosphere of the sixteen-fifties. "His tenets are dangerous," a major wrote of another rank in 1657, "maintaining perfection in this life." Pacifism and abstention from politics became dominant in the Quaker movement only after 1660.

The most obviously political religious group was that of the Fifth Monarchists, who believed that the reign of Christ upon earth was shortly to begin. This view was held by many respectable Independent divines, who drew no directly political conclusions. But for less-educated laymen, under the economic stress of the revolutionary decades, especially after the defeat of the Levellers and the dissolution of the Barebones Parliament, Fifth Monarchy became a desperately held hope. Only Christ's second coming could achieve what political action had failed to win. The duty of the elect was to eliminate hindrances to Christ's rule on earth. This often, in political terms, became "overturn, overturn, overturn," a doctrine of political anarchism. The existing state and its rulers were bad and must be rejected. In December 1653, Vavasor Powell told his congregation to go home and pray, "Lord, wilt thou have Oliver Cromwell or Jesus Christ to reign over us?" In 1657 and 1661 Fifth Monarchist risings, headed by the wine cooper Thomas Venner, threatened to overthrow the government. The sense of the imminence of a new spiritual epoch, in which God's people should be free in a new way, was one of the many Fifth Monarchist concepts which the Quakers took over.

Not all Puritans expected the millennium in the immediate future. But the essence of Puritanism as a revolutionary creed lay in the belief that God intended the betterment of man's life on earth, that men could understand God's purposes and co-operate with Him to bring them to fruition. So men's innermost wishes, if strongly enough felt, could be believed to be God's will. By a natural dialectic, those who were most convinced that they were fighting God's battles proved the most effective fighters: because they trusted God they took the very greatest care to keep their powder dry, and were ready to accept a discipline that was effective because self-imposed.

"The godly being in league with God," wrote the Puritan Thomas Gataker in all simplicity in 1626, "may have all his forces and armies for their help and assistance, whensoever need shall be." "Our duty," wrote Hugh Peter twenty years later, "will be only to look to the duty which is ours, and leave events to God, which are his." "We cannot limit God to this or that," Ireton admitted, "but certainly if we take the most probable way according to the light we have, God gives those things" their success. So men followed their consciences, with grim conviction. Many men agreed that it was their conscientious duty to oppose Charles I and Bishops: and this agreement increased their confidence that their cause was God's. But "liberty hath a sharp and double edge, fit only to be handled by just and virtuous men," said Milton. "The Providences of God are like a two-edged sword, which may be used both ways," a member of Parliament agreed in 1654. After victory agreement among the godly ceased. "All [God's] communications are reasonable and just," said the Leveller Overton; but these communications seemed different to rich and poor. The riot of conflicting sects is the measure of this tendency of the Protestant emphasis on the individual conscience to degenerate into anarchy.

There is another paradoxical element in the Puritan moral compulsion. Men fought for God's cause, and expected it to prevail because it was God's. This confidence helped to bring victory, and victory reinforced the conviction that the cause was indeed His. The humbler the agents of divine Providence, the more manifest God's favour in their success. The democratic implications of this are clear. But the doctrine could turn into one of justification by success: Cromwell and Milton came near to this at times. As divisions set in, not all were equally successful; as the divisions increased, ultimately the whole cause fell in ruins. So first the radicals, and then all the Puritans, had to ask themselves whether justification by success also meant condemnation by defeat. After the failure of the Levellers, the radical sects in their desperation first became wilder and more millennarian (Fifth Monarchists, early Quakers) and then gradually concluded that Christ's kingdom was not of this world.

After 1660 the quietist, pacifist tendency increased as Puritanism turned into nonconformity. The collapse of all his hopes forced Milton to wrestle with God in the attempt to justify His ways to man. The products of this anguish were *Paradise Lost* and *Samson Agonistes*. The former, emphasising God's justice in spite of everything, appears to end on a note of quietism and resignation: "A Paradise within thee, happier far" was a moral, not a political aim. But *Samson Agonistes,* with its emphasis on man's integrity, shouts defiance in God's face for deserting His people, and ends in reconciliation only after God has aided Samson to avenge the oppressed on the Philistines. "Calm of mind, all passion spent" is attained only after we have envisaged God's (and Milton's) cause as an undying Phoenix.

Most Puritan ministers had adopted the traditional view that God's elect were a minority, and the mass of men predestined to eternal damnation. A coercive state existed to keep the reprobate in subjection. But in order to encourage their congregations and save them from despair, they had also taught that anyone who seriously worried about his salvation probably already had sparks of divine grace at work in him. It was a short but momentous step — and

to Calvinist ministers a monstrous step — to proclaim that all men were equally eligible to receive divine grace. Walwyn and Winstanley, like Bacon, thought the Fall of Man retrievable on earth by man's efforts to master his fate: the conclusion of *Paradise Lost* suggests that man could rise to greater heights here than Adam before the Fall. Men of property had hitherto tacitly assumed that the laws which restrained the ungodly had been drafted by godly men, and were administered by godly men. But the Levellers and Diggers thought the corruption of fallen man was equally obvious in the old ruling classes and in those who replaced them during the Civil War. A wider suffrage, annual elections, and the unchangeable "'fundamentals" of the Agreement of the People were designed to preserve rulers from the tendency of power to corrupt.

Far-reaching consequences followed. If there is a spark of the divine in all men, preaching should not be a clerical monopoly. No spoken or printed word should be suppressed, lest God's truth be lost. If all men were equal before Christ, should they not also be equal before the law? Should they not have the vote? Parliament had appealed to public opinion by the Grand Remonstrance in 1641; the Independent dissenting brethren in the Westminster Assembly had used the press to appeal to Parliament and public in 1644; three years later the Levellers appealed from "the degenerate representative body, the Commons of England . . . to the body represented, the free people." Where was this to stop? Was toleration to extend "to debar any kind of restraint on anything that any will call religion?" Ireton asked. If not — who was to decide where the lines were to be drawn?

The power of the Church had broken down with the abolition of the High Commission. Church lands were taxed in the same way as lay property; Church courts ceased to function. In 1650 compulsory attendance at one's parish church was legally abolished, provided one attended at some place of worship. The proviso was unenforceable. This recognised a major achievement: liberation of the common man from parson and squire. It marked a quite new type of freedom for those hitherto unaccustomed to freedom of any sort. It was too good to last.

Religious toleration, then, posed in a new form the problem of discipline. The Presbyterians and their supporters had not abolished Church courts in order to set natural men free to follow their sinful impulses, but in order to submit them to a more effective control. Yet the Presbyterian disciplinary system was never effective. Cromwell's state Church had a system of Triers and Ejectors of ministers, who, Baxter said, "saved many a congregation from ignorant, ungodly, drunken teachers." But it had no discipline, no courts. A horrid vacuum remained. There was grave danger that the lower orders might be able to do what they liked, within the limits of the common law. When Bishops had been closely connected with the government in Laud's time, the hierarchy of Church courts had acted as a link between central and local government. The Major-Generals restored such a link, attempted to fill the vacuum, to re-establish some standards of conduct. We should not exaggerate this part of their activities: they were far more often concerned with security than godliness when they prohibited race-meetings or cock-fightings at which Cavaliers might foregather, or when they closed disorderly alehouses. When they enforced, for example, Sabbath observance they were only putting into effect Parliamentary legislation of the sixteen-twenties which Stuart governments had ignored. The idea that they imposed gloomy godliness on a merrie nation is a post-Restoration myth.

But there was a vacuum. In the sixteen-fifties groups of ministers got together to build up a Presbyterian system from below, within the framework of the Cromwellian state Church. We know from Baxter, the moving spirit in Worcestershire,

that their main motive was concern about the behaviour of the lower orders. But a disciplinary system without state power behind it was about as effective as voluntary maintenance of ministers. Here is one powerful reason why conservatives supported the restoration of episcopacy in 1660 Bunyan learnt from Justices of the Peace and judges in 1660 that for them the Restoration meant that tinkers and other mechanic laymen should return to their callings and leave divinity to the clergy. In 1640 Baxter had wanted episcopacy to be abolished. But in April 1660 he told the House of Commons, "The question is not, whether Bishops or no, but whether discipline or none." He was not alone in this view. Throughout this period the Commons always opposed toleration fiercely. When the Quaker James Nayler symbolically rode into Bristol in 1656 with women strewing palms before him, Parliament imposed savage penalties on him. Not only Nayler, not only the Quakers, but toleration itself (and the Major-Generals themselves) was on trial. The episode was an essential preliminary to the restriction of toleration and restoration of Parliamentary monarchy by the Petition and Advice.

The tolerance of even a Cromwell or a Milton did not extend to Papists. For this the reasons were largely political. Papists were regarded as agents of a foreign power. They had solidly supported Charles in the Civil War, and after the capture of the King's papers at Naseby he was known to have planned Irish intervention on a large scale. This helps to explain, though not to excuse, the Commonwealth's savagely repressive policy in Ireland, which only Levellers opposed. Hostility to Papists was not a monopoly of the Puritans. In 1640 a group of condemned men in Newgate gaol had conscientious scruples about being hanged unless seven condemned priests whom the King was trying to save were hanged with them. The Parliamentarians also refused toleration to "Prelatists," for similar political reasons. The vast majority of ministers

accepted the ecclesiastical changes and retained their livings throughout the forties
and fifties: the small minority of Laudian
clergy formed one of the main Royalist resistance groups. The future Bishop Jeremy

Taylor wrote a moving plea for toleration
in 1647; but this doctrine was not acted
upon when the Anglican hierarchy was restored in 1660. . . .

The Achievements

MAURICE ASHLEY

Maurice Ashley (1907–   ), historian and journalist, was educated at
New College, Oxford, and upon graduation served as historical research assistant to Sir Winston Churchill. After having served on the editorial staffs of *The
Manchester Guardian*, *The Times*, and *Britain Today*, he became editor of *The
Listener* and *BBC Television Review* in 1958. President of the Cromwell Association since 1961, Professor Ashley is the author of numerous articles, reviews,
and books. Among his outstanding works are: *Financial and Commercial Policy
under the Cromwellian Protectorate*, *Cromwell's Generals*, and *The Greatness
of Oliver Cromwell*.

WHAT DID the Puritan Revolution
achieve? Did it in fact achieve
anything at all? In our standard history
books the question is surprisingly little discussed. The year 1660 is taken almost as a
closed frontier in historical time or a safety-
curtain lowered after a play that is best forgotten. It was a revolution that failed, had
it not? For King Charles II was restored un-
conditionally and by the very army that
had once followed Oliver Cromwell. Nothing of importance, we are instructed, was
retained out of all the legislation and political activity of the years between 1642,
when King Charles I left his capital, and
May 1660, when his son returned there.
Most of the conclusions that are offered us
come in negatives: Cromwell "had not succeeded in making Puritanism admirable to
the majority of Englishmen" or "England
had repudiated the Puritan attempt to enforce strict morality by the use of the army."

It would hardly be credible that this revolution, in which so much blood and fire
and passion were expended, should have
left no mark whatever upon British history.
It would be astonishing if all the political
experiments, all the philosophical thinking,
all the religious exuberance, all the written
constitutions and different governments of
those eighteen years had made no impression whatsoever upon the minds of men; or
if the character of Oliver Cromwell, which,
even upon the tercentenary of his death,
divides the judgments of historians and
arouses journalists to display contradictory
opinions, contributed nothing to the moulding of later society.

To take the obvious points first. It is not
entirely true that the legislation of the Interregnum left no traces in the statute book.
To give two examples: important reforms of
the law (which Cromwell had so much at
heart) were retained; it was confirmed that

From Maurice Ashley, *Oliver Cromwell and the Puritan Revolution* (London, 1958). Reprinted by
permission of The English Universities Press Limited, London, pp. 173–183.

in the future the language of the Common Law courts should be English and not French or dog Latin, and also that a defendant might enter a general plea of "not guilty," and so be able to join issue at once without preliminary production of evidence in bar of an action. Secondly, the series of Navigation Acts introduced after the Restoration were merely an extension of the navigation laws carried through and enforced during the Interregnum. They had the same objects: to enable shipowners and shippers to compete more effectively with their chief commercial rivals, the Dutch, in the carrying trade, and to promote Britain's business intercourse with her colonies. Maybe none of these Acts were soundly designed for their purpose (though in the twentieth century we are less dogmatic about Protection than our grandfathers), but at least they exemplify a striking continuation of policy.

Among other concrete survivals from the Interregnum are two of our most famous historical regiments, the Coldstream Guards — direct descendants of the Ironsides — and the Grenadier Guards. The greatness of the British Navy may also be said to date largely from the Cromwellian era; for, if it was founded by King Henry VIII and built up by Queen Elizabeth I, it won some of its most notable victories in the Dutch and Spanish wars. Nearly half the Lord Protector's revenue was spent upon the navy; it was the foundation which allowed Britain to become a great power in the seventeenth century, and from the time of Robert Blake it kept a continuous station in the Mediterranean. Blake and Monk in their different ways were commanders of great ability. After the Restoration, Monk, Penn, Batten, and other naval officers continued to serve the monarchy and uphold the Commonwealth traditions. The new tactics, principally invented by Blake and Monk, were pursued when war came, and it was naval prestige, won during the Protectorate, that encouraged King Charles II's government to try conclusions with the

Dutch, though less successfully than before.

It was not only at sea that the services of Commonwealth administrators were employed. Indeed, it was under Cromwell that capable men with something approaching a Civil Service cast of mind were employed by the executive, instead of rich men who bought their offices and left most of the duties to their underlings. The alliance with France was affirmed, the wars with the Dutch resumed, the connection with Portugal was strengthened. Some of the colonial conquests from Spain were maintained. Jamaica, it has been said, became the "pet colony" of the Restoration. Thence were exported coffee, sugar, and pepper, and the island became an excellent market for English manufactured goods. Buccaneering, as was anticipated during the Interregnum, became a profitable industry, and from Jamaica the headquarters of Spanish trade in Central America was sacked. But not all the conquests of the Cromwellian era were retained; the union with Scotland (provided for in "The Instrument of Government") was abandoned; in October 1662 Dunkirk was sold to France, a step that was very unpopular at the time and helped to bring about the downfall of King Charles II's minister, the first Earl of Clarendon, who was believed to have advised the sale. Acadia was surrendered to the Dutch in 1667, although later it was regained. The gradual decline in English prestige abroad during the reigns of King Charles II and King James II, a fact to which attention was first drawn in a famous pamphlet by Andrew Marvell, who had served under Thurloe during the Protectorate, was extremely damaging to the Stuarts; even the most loyal Royalists looked back sadly to the "great days of Oliver." It was not until the Dutchman, King William III, ascended the throne in 1689 that the rulers of England and France again became equals.

Although the restoration of King Charles II was unconditional, the intention of parliament was to return to the constitutional position of 1642 and not of 1640. Though no mention was made of legislation passed during the first year of the Long Parliament, it was tacitly and implicitly confirmed; for only the later ordinances of the Long Parliament, which had not received the assent of King Charles I, were specifically declared invalid. Thus the Tudor Royal courts, the dubious methods of raising taxes, the imprisonments without cause shown, and other exercises in the use of prerogative power were all swept away. Moreover, though the Triennial Act, which Oliver Cromwell had helped to introduce, was repealed, a new one required the King to summon a fresh parliament three years after a previous one had been dissolved. King Charles II could, therefore, only tax his subjects with parliament's consent; justice was confined to the Common Law courts and the Court of Chancery; and in effect the jurisdiction of the ecclesiastical courts was much more limited than it had been before the civil wars.

The privileges of the House of Commons were now finally recognized by the Crown. A historian has recently written that at the Restoration,

the old unity of "King in Parliament" was replaced by a new trinity of "Kings, Lords, and Commons," and the replacement was perhaps only unchallenged because it was clothed in a restoration.

The growing independence of the House of Commons was accepted. The Long Parliament or Pensionary Parliament of King Charles II's reign which, when it met, was enthusiastically Royalist, became, after the initial failures of the government in foreign and domestic policy, hostile in temper ten years later, even though its original membership had not been substantially changed. Constitutional advance is, after all, always dictated by political facts. The structure of parliament was probably not materially altered. King Charles II may

have tried to pick his later parliaments, but he did not dare to defy them indefinitely as his father had done. King James II found he was unable to pick or pack a parliament which he needed to promote his own religious ends. Both men were forewarned by the fate of their father. The bloody revolution of 1649 was the prelude to the bloodless revolution of forty years later, when King James II preferred to escape in a yacht to France rather than to fight another civil war. If it is true, as Mr. David Ogg has written, that in some respects Charles II was a constitutional monarch, that was because he never forgot that parliament had beaten his father and he did not intend to go into exile again.

Charles II was an agreeable, accessible, highly intelligent man. No one can say with confidence, any more than one can say of any man, that he was completely devoid of moral principles, but the behaviour of his Court set lax standards. When he married his Portuguese Queen, he at once insisted that his principal mistress should be made her Lady of the Bedchamber. He promoted men not because of their inherent capacities, but, as in the case of the second Duke of Buckingham, because they were amusing companions. He winked at piracies and robberies if the pirates or robbers happened to entertain him. Like the rest of the Stuarts, he had little sense of personal loyalty; he was indolent and extravagant, and his gay Court was a centre of vice. It has often been pointed out that there were many respectable and devoted men and women among the servants of King Charles II, but the Court set the tone to society, and corruption flourished in the administration in a way that it never did when Oliver Cromwell lived in Whitehall.

If the pattern of society changed during the reign of King Charles II, the Church was even more violently affected by the Restoration. The many Presbyterians who had assisted in bringing back the King had assumed that a place would be found for them in the ecclesiastical settlement. In the autumn of 1656 a scheme for combining Presbyterian and episcopal government, invented by Archbishop Ussher of Armagh, had been published, and many Presbyterians hoped that as the price for their aid they would be comprehended within the Church of England. In fact, it was the Laudians, headed by Dr. Gilbert Sheldon, Bishop of London, who, having carefully prepared the way during the Interregnum, triumphed after Charles II's return. William Laud, the High Church Archbishop of Canterbury, who had been beheaded on Tower Hill in 1645, like Samson, slew more Puritans by his death than he ever did in his life. The resurgent Laudianism of the Restoration was, however, devoid of any social or political content; it was a purely ecclesiastical victory. At the Savoy conference, held in the Bishop of London's lodgings in 1660, the Presbyterian leaders, badly led, were outmaneuvered, and by the Act of Uniformity of 1661, a revised Book of Common Prayer was imposed upon all clergy, who were compelled to sign a declaration promising to adopt the new book and to repudiate the Solemn League and Covenant. Thus the Presbyterians, together with the dissenters or sectarians, were driven out of the Church. It has been estimated that 2,000 out of 10,000 parochial clergy resigned their livings, and when, on St. Bartholomew's Day, 1662, they gave up their benefices, nonconformity took permanent shape.

The Act of Uniformity was buttressed by a number of other measures known collectively as "the Clarendon Code." By the Conventicle Act, if five or more persons met for religious purposes the meeting was declared illegal, and transportation was the penalty for the third offence. By the Five Mile Act, all men in holy orders who did not take the prescribed oaths were forbidden to teach or preach in corporate towns. Another Act allowed constables to break into houses where it was suspected that nonconformists met. The reason for this panic legislation was because the govern-

ment feared that the nonconformists were plotting another revolution under the cover of religion. This was far from being the case. But a heavy blow had been delivered against the Presbyterians; some of them joined the Church of England, took the oaths, and created a kind of Low Church movement. Others allied with their old enemies, the Independents or Congregationalists. And, in reaction against the violence of both sides in the former religious conflict, a Broad or Latitudinarian movement began in the Church, with which a former brother-in-law of Oliver Cromwell, Dr. Wilkins, Bishop of Chester, was associated.

Though dissent continued to flourish in those areas where the magistrates were sympathetic and therefore did not strictly enforce the Clarendon Code, undoubtedly the Code was damaging to the nonconformists. According to one estimate, there were in the reign of King Charles II only about 150,000 of them left out of a total population of over five millions. When one considers how Puritanism had coloured the whole life of the country in the Cromwellian era, this is a strikingly low figure, if it can be believed. But whatever they lacked in numbers, the nonconformists made up in tenacity and variety; when the Grand Duke of Tuscany visited the country he was astounded at the diversity of religious beliefs. Naturally, one must not underestimate the strain to which they were subjected by the persecution under the Clarendon Code. A recent writer on Puritanism in that period has hazarded the opinion that it injured them permanently, and that, after the smoke of battle cleared in 1689, their "old resiliency of spirit" had disappeared. But if the religious side of nonconformity suffered, its political, economic and, above all, social influence remained strong, if indirect. Though the nonconformists could take no part in public life, they formed a pressure group as early as the eighteenth century. Above all, the Puritan Revolution brought to birth the nonconformists' conscience, which ripened during the struggles under the later Stuarts,

ame to maturity in the reign of Queen
Anne, and permeated middle-class society,
regardless of creed, in the reign of Queen
Victoria.

The severity of the Clarendon Code was
explained by the fear of the government
that the dissenters might take advantage of
the confusion caused by the second Dutch
war (1664–7), the Great Plague (1665),
and the Great Fire of London (1666), to
plot a fresh revolution; but they were never
sufficiently powerful or united to contem-
plate any such action. True, they were disappointed, especially after the promises of
indulgence given by the King himself in
the early years of his reign, that they were
not allowed to attend their chapels peace-
fully under their own ministers, while the
Presbyterians believed that they had been
betrayed. But in so far as republican plotting continued after the Restoration, it was
in the spirit of Haselrigg, Ludlow, and the
keener secular politicians, and was not specifically religious in its inspiration.

King Charles II declared himself to be
a Roman Catholic upon his deathbed in
1685, and his brother had long been an
open adherent of that religion when he
came to the throne as King James II. It
was a remarkable historical volte-face. That
less than thirty years after Oliver Cromwell was buried and much more than a century after Queen Mary I died, a new Roman Catholic ruler should succeed peace-
fully to the thrones of both England and
Scotland postulated a degree of religious
apathy and a weakening in the national
character that contrasted strangely with all
the passion and excitement of the Interregnum.

Yet a flash of the old spirit soon disclosed
that whatever promises the new King had
given to his parliament, and however ac-
quiescent the official Church of England
might be in turning the other cheek, this
state of affairs could not endure. For the
ninth Earl of Argyll landed in Scotland
with a handful of followers and tried to
arouse the ardour of the Presbyterians,
while the Duke of Monmouth, the King's

illegitimate nephew, pitched camp in Lyme
in Dorset, after sailing from Holland, and
planned to arouse the West of England
and capture Bristol as a base. Here, in fact,
the dissenters rallied to the standard of the
"Protestant Duke" in large numbers.
Crowds of uncompromising nonconformist
tradesmen and peasants offered their services in the very area which had been most
persistently Royalist during the civil wars.
The motives of these men in joining Monmouth were religious and not economic.
The two rebellions came too soon and were
crushed. But nonconformity had been
awakened out of its passive acceptance of
persecution by the old anti-papal war-cries
that had pierced the air in the sixteen-for-
ties. Soon the ruling classes were to unite
almost solidly against the Jesuit-inspired
ambitions of King James II. Though in his
Declaration of Indulgence of 1687 the
King tried to draw over the nonconformists
to his side, the Marquis of Halifax, who
had once been the protector of the rights
of James Stuart when his brother had been
upon the throne, riposted with a famous
pamphlet, entitled "A Letter to a Dis-
senter," in which he argued that liberty and
infallibility were contradictory and that
the nonconformists, rather than trust the
promises of the Declaration of Indulgence,
ought to await "the next probable revolution." When seven bishops were sent to the
Tower of London to await trial for seditious
libel because they had refused for specified
reasons to permit the reading of King James
II's second Declaration of Indulgence in the
churches, many nonconformists actually assured them of their sympathy. Thus a virtually united nation drove the Roman Catholic King from his throne and achieved a
revolution without a battle.

But if the nonconformists did not enter
into conspiracies before the reign of King
James II, there was a link between the
men who had fought King Charles I and
those who destroyed his son. A group of
underground conspirators, some of whom
had been imprisoned during the Clarendon
régime, had emerged to associate, first with

the second Duke of Buckingham whose "cabal" was said to include Cromwell's famous chaplain, Dr. John Owen, and caused Samuel Pepys to report: "Some say we are carried in Oliver's bucket." Later this group tried to exclude James Stuart from the throne and even to revive a republican movement. It was concerned in the so-called Rye House Plot (1683) against King Charles II, and later the Duke of Monmouth's rising. Some of these conspirators were caught and executed, but a few survivors fled to Holland and returned with William of Orange at the Glorious Revolution.

The Revolution Settlement in 1689 comprised an Act of Toleration which, in effect, acquiesced in organized nonconformity by permitting the suspension of the penal code against dissenting meetings and granting concessions to dissenting ministers. The Bill of Rights, to which King William III gave his assent in the same year, further reinforced the powers of parliament and reduced those of the Crown. It also laid it down that henceforward no monarch might be a Roman Catholic or marry a Roman Catholic. It was perhaps the greatest constitutional document in modern history and, like the revolution of 1649, it owed its origins to the misdeeds of a Stuart King.

After the pendulum had swung back in the early years of Charles II's reign, the settlement of 1689 thus completed the constitutional revolution of the seventeenth century. The Bill of Rights repaired some of the inadequacies of the legislation of 1641. Possibly if King Charles I had agreed to the same sort of restrictions upon his prerogative and if the parliamentary leaders could have trusted him, that settlement might have been attained earlier. As it was, the execution of King Charles I and the experiments of the Protectorate produced a Royalist reaction, but at the same time afforded a warning to the aristocracy and wealthier ruling classes of what might happen again if they did not this time join together to depose a monarch who at-

tempted to dispense with parliament and rule by his personal powers. The importance of the Puritan Revolution in British history cannot be understood except in the context of the settlement in 1689.

It is sometimes said that this revolution was an historical aberration which it is best patriotically to slide over, an affront to the ideal of the peaceful and orderly constitutional progress which appeals to placid Englishmen. In the same way, Oliver Cromwell has never been accepted as a national hero in the same senses as, say the first William Pitt, Earl of Chatham, the Duke of Wellington, or Lord Nelson. Not even a great soldier, some of his critics observe, for other men fought his battles for him, and anyhow he did not fight French or Germans but the Scots, the Irish, and his fellow countrymen. Disregarding the testimonies of his own letters and his own servants, his humaneness is denied because he treated the ancestors of the Sinn Feiners as badly as the Black-and-Tans. The Irish hate him because he conquered them, the Scots because he subdued them, the aesthetes because he collected horses instead of paintings, the Roman Catholics because he did not believe in the Mass, the Socialists because he suppressed the Levellers, the Liberals because for a short spell he ruled as a military dictator, the Conservatives because he killed a King.

But history need not be written in such simple terms, and Cromwell should be seen not through the coloured spectacles of our own emotions, but in the glaring light of his own times. One may conclude by quoting the words of a recent writer, not a professional historian but a detached observer:

Cromwell's claim to greatness is that within the limitations set him by the people he had to deal with and the events with which he had to contend, he pursued a policy which apart from restoring our national reputation abroad, saved England at home from the extremes of bloody repression and deepening chaos.

Cromwell neither betrayed, nor did he fulfil, the ideals of the Puritan Revolution. He tried and failed to make of Puritanism a political instrument. He was forced to acquiesce in an attempt, which failed, to impose upon England the Puritan pattern of social behaviour. But both these failures were contained within the frame of a larger success. A new principle of Government had been asserted; a new standard of behaviour had been established. For good or ill the religious and secular principles of the Reformation had been consolidated, and were never again to be seriously challenged. The defeat of James II had been assured thirty years before he ascended the throne; England had been secured from the Counter-Reformation, and from all its implications of bloodshed, misery and obscurantism.

Thus the spirit and achievements of Oliver Cromwell were active elements in the revolution of 1688; they gave their impulse to a permanent form of English institutions; they largely attained their long-term objectives; and they may be said to have entered effectively into the making of modern England.

SUGGESTIONS FOR ADDITIONAL READING

Any study of the mid-seventeenth century should begin with Godfrey Davies, *Bibliography of British History, Stuart Period, 1603–1714* (Oxford, 1928), and *The Early Stuarts, 1603–1660* (Oxford, 1937) by the same author. Mary Keeler is in the process of editing a new edition of Davies' *Bibliography*, bringing it up to date. The work of Samuel R. Gardiner and Sir Charles Firth is indispensable for the period. Gardiner's *The History of the Great Civil War, 1642–1649*, 3 vols. (London, 1886–91); and *History of the Commonwealth and Protectorate*, 3 vols. (London, 1894–1901) are unsurpassed. C. H. Firth brought Gardiner's work to a close in his *The Last Years of the Protectorate*, 2 vols. (London, 1909). Firth's work in turn was brought to a conclusion by Godfrey Davies, *The Restoration of Charles II, 1658–1660* (San Marino, California, 1955). Several bibliographical essays have been written which are valuable to a study of this period, among them Perez Zagorin, "English History, 1558–1640: A Bibliographical Survey," *English Historical Review*, LXXVIII (1963), and Paul H. Hardacre, "Writings of Oliver Cromwell Since 1929," *Journal of Modern History*, XXXIII (1961).

Documents of the period are plentiful: S. R. Gardiner's *Constitutional Documents, 1625–60*, 2 vols. (London, 1889); C. H. Firth and R. S. Rait, *Acts and Ordinances of the Interregnum, 1642–60* (London, 1911) are still basic. The Sutherland manuscripts in the Historical Manuscripts Commission series; State Papers, Domestic Series, and State Papers, Foreign, in the Public Records Office; John Rushworth, *Historical Selections*, 7 vols. (London, 1659–1701) are all invaluable. There are actually two collections of debates: *Parliamentary History of England*, 24 vols. (London, 1751–62), good for the period 1642–60; and *The Parliamentary History of England*, ed. William Cobbett, 36 vols. (1806–20).

The seventeenth-century commentators are worth reading in spite of what would seem strong bias. The best edition of Edward Hyde, Earl of Clarendon, *The History of the Great Rebellion*, is that edited by W. D. Macray (Oxford, 1888), in six volumes. A fine commentary on Clarendon is Charles H. Firth, "Clarendon's History of the Rebellion," *English Historical Review*, XIX (1904). Lucy B. Wormald, *Clarendon: Politics, History, and Religion* (Cambridge, 1951) is a short recent edition. J. H. Lister, *Life and Administration of Edward, First Earl of Clarendon*, 3 vols. (London, 1837–38) is not as good on Cromwell and the Revolution as is the *Rebellion*. Lucy Hutchinson, *Memoirs of the Life of Colonel Hutchinson*, is available in an Everyman's Library edition, as is Richard Baxter's *Autobiography*. Frederick Powicke, *A Life of the Reverend Richard Baxter, 1615–1691* (London, 1924) supplements the *Autobiography*. A recent work is Richard Schlatter, *Richard Baxter and Puritan Politics* (New Brunswick, New Jersey, 1961). The best life of John Milton is the deservedly famous *The Life of John Milton*, 6 vols. (London, 1859–1894 by David Masson, although several recent works are quite good. F. E. Hutchinson, *Milton and the English Mind* (London, 1947) available in paperback and Don M. Wolfe, *Milton in the Puritan Revolution* (London, 1941), less a biography than the others, contains valuable insights into Milton's political activities. *The Memoirs of Edmund Ludlow*, edited by C. H. Firth, 2 vols. (Oxford, 1894) presents the strict Republican point of view.

The Royalist voice is heard in *The Diary of John Evelyn*, edited by E. S. De Beer (Oxford, 1955); C. H. Firth, "The Royalists during the Protectorate," *English Historical Review*, LII (1937); Paul H. Hardacre, *The Royalists during the Puritan Revolution* (The Hague, 1956); and David Underdown, *Royalists Conspiracy in Eng-*

land, 1649–1660 (New Haven, 1960). Two works, M. F. Keeler, *The Long Parliament, 1640–1641: A Bibliographical Study of Its Members* (Philadelphia, 1954); and Douglas O. Brunton and Donald H. Pennington, *Members of the Long Parliament* (Cambridge, Mass., 1954) investigate the membership of that parliament. A brief commentary on biography in general is Charles F. Mullett's *Biography as History: Men and Movements in Europe Since 1500* (New York, 1963). The *Dictionary of National Biography*, 22 vols. (London, 1908–09) is, of course, invaluable for any study of the leading personages of the seventeenth century.

Anyone who would understand Oliver Cromwell should begin with Wilbur C. Abbott's, *A Bibliography of Oliver Cromwell* (Cambridge, Mass., 1929), supplemented in the same author's *Writings and Speeches of Oliver Cromwell*, Vol. IV (Cambridge, Mass., 1947), "Addenda to Bibliography," bringing it down to 1944. Professor Abbott enumerates over 3,500 items on the Lord Protector. Although dated, Thomas Carlyle's *The Letters and Speeches of Oliver Cromwell* (London, 1854) is still valuable and readable. The biographies of Oliver Cromwell are plentiful and represent the Lord Protector in varying degrees from saint to tyrant. Two nineteenth-century views by distinguished foreigners are Francis Guizot, *The History of Oliver Cromwell and the English Commonwealth* (Paris, 1826), and Leopold von Ranke, *History of England During the Seventeenth Century* (London, 1875). Both of these men based a reasonably impersonal view on dispatches from the Foreign Offices. Guizot defended Cromwell and identified with him in light of his own experience as a statesman under Louis Phillippe; Von Ranke admired Cromwell for his energetic foreign policy, although both historians felt that his religious zeal was insincere. Later historians were chiefly concerned with Cromwell either as a soldier or a dictator. At the turn of the century Gardiner and Firth turned their attention to the Lord

Protector: C. H. Firth, *Oliver Cromwell and the Rule of the Puritans in England* (London, 1901), and S. R. Gardiner *Oliver Cromwell* (London, 1899) and *Cromwell's Place in History* (London, 1897) by the same author.

In the eyes of his biographers, at least in the 1930's, Cromwell was transformed into a dictator. There were obvious comparisons between Cromwell and Mussolini and Hitler. Mary T. Blauvelt, *A Dictator's Tragedy* (New York, 1937), and Maurice Ashley, *The Conservative Dictator* (London, 1937) were both concerned with the political activities of Cromwell. Additional biographies were written: Ernest Barker, *Oliver Cromwell and the English People* (Cambridge, 1937); John Buchan, *Oliver Cromwell* (London, 1934); C. V. Wedgwood, *Oliver Cromwell* (London, 1939), saw the Lord Protector as "a perplexed Atlas." For a Christian view there is a biography of Cromwell, *The Lord Protector* (London, 1955) by Rev. Robert S. Paul, who emphasizes Cromwell's religious conscience. Writing in the 1950's Maurice Ashley reevaluates Cromwell in two works: *The Greatness of Oliver Cromwell* (London, 1957) emphasizing Cromwell's religious toleration, and *Oliver Cromwell and the Puritan Revolution* (London, 1958). Christopher Hill, *Oliver Cromwell, 1658–1958* (London, 1958) is an economic view. The most recent work is by Peter Young, *Oliver Cromwell* (London, 1963).

Cromwell's military career has been the subject of much scholarly research and one might begin with C. V. Wedgwood's *The Great Rebellion* in two volumes: *The King's Peace, 1637–1641* (London, 1955) and *The King's War, 1641–1647* (London, 1958). These volumes contain more than the titles would indicate. *The Regimental History of Cromwell's Army*, 2 vols. (Oxford, 1940) by Charles H. Firth and Godfrey Davies contains a wealth of biographical information. Maurice Ashley, *Cromwell's Generals* (London, 1954) supplements this and is extremely good for biographical sketches of the officers. A. H

Woolrych, *Battles of the Civil War* (New York, 1961) is a recent account of military strategy. Several articles contribute to this area. Godfrey Davies, "The Army of the Eastern Association, 1644–5," *English Historical Review*, XLVI (1931); D. E. Kennedy, "The English Naval Revolt of 1648," *English Historical Review*, LXXVII (1962). Christopher Hill, "Recent Interpretations of the Civil War," *History*, XII (1956) is a bibliographical essay on the Civil War.

Other military figures have their defenders or critics also. M. A. Gibb, *The Lord General: A Life of Thomas Fairfax* (London, 1938); W. H. Dawson, *Cromwell's Understudy: The Life of Thomas Fairfax* (London, 1938) is very hard on Cromwell. R. W. Ramsey, *Henry Ireton* (London, 1949) a good biography of Cromwell's son-in-law. James Berry and S. G. Lee, *A Cromwellian Major General: The Career of Colonel James Berry* (Oxford, 1938); C. E. Lucas Phillips, *Cromwell's Captain* (London, 1938); A. S. P. Woodhouse, *Puritanism and Liberty* (Chicago, 1951) contains the army debates from the Clarke manuscripts with a fine introduction by Professor Woodhouse; A. L. Leach *The History of the Civil War in Pembrokeshire and on Its Borders* (London, 1937); and Godfrey Davies "The Army and the Downfall of Richard Cromwell," *Huntington Library Bulletin*, VII (1935) are still valuable. The booklet in this series edited by Philip A. M. Taylor, *The Origins of the English Civil War* (Boston, 1960) should be consulted for further reading.

The history of the Protectorate reveals Cromwell's basic conservatism in economic affairs. R. H. Tawney's monumental work, *Religion and the Rise of Capitalism* (New York, 1926) will remain a classic in its field. His very provocative essay in *Economic History Review*, XI (1941), "The Rise of the Gentry, 1558–1640," touched off quite a controversy. Hugh R. Trevor-Roper "The Gentry, 1540–1640," *Economic History Review*, Supplements (I, 1953) criticizes Tawney's use of the concept "gentry." Trever-Roper's "The General Crisis of the Seventeenth Century" *Past and Present*, XVI (1959) stimulated Tawney's defenders to answer him in "Trevor-Roper's 'General Crisis'" *Past and Present*, XVIII (1960). Maurice Ashley, *Financial and Commercial Policy under the Cromwellian Protectorate*, 2nd edition (London, 1962) is very good. Also available are: Perez Zagorin, "The Social Interpretation of the English Revolution," *Journal of Economic History*, XIX (1959); T. S. Willan, "Trade between England and Russia," *English Historical Review*, LXIII (1948); Menna Pretwich, "Diplomacy and Trade Under the Protectorate," *Journal of Modern History*, XXII (1950); Michael Roberts, "Cromwell and the Baltic," *English Historical Review*, LXXVI (1961). H. F. Kearney, "Puritanism, Capitalism and the Scientific Revolution," *Past and Present*, XXVIII (1964) and H. Habakkuk, "The Sale of Confiscated Property during the Interregnum," *Economic History Review*, XV (1962–1963).

The Marxist view has been ably presented by a number of historians, chiefly Christopher Hill. In Professor Hill's *The English Revolution* (London, 1940), written as a Marxist textbook, he attempts to show that the Revolution was the "showdown" between capitalism and feudalism. The same general theme is found in his *The Century of Revolution, 1603–1714* (London, 1961), and *Intellectual Origins of the English Revolution* (Oxford, 1965). Hill's "Soviet Interpretations of the Interregnum" *The Economic History Review*, VIII (1938) represents the views of Soviet historians; "Church Marx and History" *Spectator*, Vol. 199 (1957); "English Revolution and Brotherhood of Man," *Science and Society*, XVIII (1954) are other valuable contributions by Professor Hill. Eduard Bernstein *Cromwell and Communism* (London, 1930) is available in paperback. Additional reading on this topic can be found in *Protestantism and Capitalism*, Problems in European Civilization (Boston, 1959.)

Anyone attempting to understand the

Puritan revolt might consult several basic works: John T. McNeill, *The History and Character of Calvinism* (New York, 1954); Marshall M. Knappen, *Tudor Puritanism: A Chapter in the History of Idealism* (Chicago, 1939) contains excellent background material on the Stuart period. Perry Miller, *The New England Mind: The Seventeenth Century* (New York, 1939) is another phase of Puritanism. See also J. S. Flynn, *The Influence of Puritanism in the Political and Religious Thought of England* (New York, 1920); Wilbur K. Jordan, *The Development of Religious Toleration in England,* Vol. 2. (Cambridge, Mass., 1940); William Haller, *The Rise of Puritanism* (New York, 1938) and *Liberty and Reformation in the Puritan Revolution* (New York, 1955) by the same author. Leonard J. Trinterud, "The Origins of Puritanism" *Church History,* XX (1961); C. H. George, "A Social Interpretation of English Puritanism," *Journal of Modern History,* XXV (1953); E. W. Kirby, "The Lay Feoffees: A Study in Militant Puritanism," *Journal of Modern History,* XIV (1942); Haller's *Tracts on Liberty in the Puritan Revolution* (New York, 1934) reproduces nineteen important pamphlets in full and in facsimile. *Godfrey Davies,* "Puritan versus Arminian," *Huntington Library Bulletin,* VI (1934) contends that the term"Arminian" is loosely used to designate the whole Laudian position. An overall explanation of the Lord Protector's religious view is G. F. Nuttall, *The Holy Spirit in Puritan Faith and Experience* (Oxford, 1946).

An account of religion in the army is Leo F. Solt, *Saints in Arms* (Stanford, California, 1959) and an older work by D. W. Petegorsky, *Left Wing Democracy in The English Civil War* (London, 1940). See also William Haller and Godfrey Davies, eds., *The Leveller Tracts, 1647–1653* (New York, 1944); G. H. Sabine, ed.,

The Works of Gerrard Winstanley (Ithaca, N.Y., 1941); D. M. Wolfe, ed., *Leveller Manifestoes of the Puritan Revolution* (New York, 1944); H. Holorenshaw, *The Levellers and the English Revolution* (London, 1939); Alan Cole, "The Quakers and the English Revolution," *Past and Present,* X (1956); R. C. Latham, "English Revolutionary Thought, 1640–1660," *History,* XXX (1945); Raymond P. Stearns, *The Strenuous Puritan: Hugh Peter, 1598–1660* (Urbana, Illinois, 1954); William M. Lamont, "William Prynne," *History Today,* XI (1961); Robert S. Bosher, *The Making of the Restoration Settlement* (London, 1951) emphasizes the Laudian influence. *The English Presbyterians and the Stuart Restoration, 1648–1663* (Philadelphia, 1965) by George R. Abernathy, Jr., is a new and valuable addition.

From a constitutional standpoint C. H. Firth, "Cromwell and the Expulsion of the Long Parliament in 1653," *English Historical Review,* XIII (1893) indicates that Cromwell went with the tide of army opinion. See also "Secretary Thurloe on the relations of England and Holland," *English Historical Review,* XXXVIII (1923) by the same author. A later work on Thurloe is D. F. Underdown, "Sir Richard Willys and Secretary Thurloe," *English Historical Review,* LXIX (1954). See also Trevor-Roper, "Oliver Cromwell and His Parliaments," in Richard Pares and A. J. P. Taylor, *Essays Presented to Sir Lewis Namier* (London, 1956); and Vernon F. Snow, "Parliamentary Reapportionment Proposals in the Puritan Revolution," *English Historical Review,* LXXIV (1959). A more general field of evidence, and one largely unworked, exists in the numerous broadsides, tracts, and theological works on the time. They often throw a useful light on economic and ecclesiastical problems as well as on political policy.